Compiled by Peter C. Kesling

First Edition, First Printing

Copyright 2002
by Peter C. Kesling Foundation—La Porte, Indiana
ISBN 0-9717455-0-1

Published by
by Peter C. Kesling Foundation
La Porte, Indiana

For more information or to order this book, contact Door Prairie Auto Museum,
P.O. Box 1771, La Porte, IN 46352-1771; (219) 326-1337; fax: (219) 326-1437;
e-mail: dpmuseum@csinet.net; web site www.dpautomuseum.com

2002 Reprint of *The Mad Doctor's Drive*
with permission of the Estate of Ralph Nading Hill.

Unless otherwise noted, original photographs on the following pages
courtesy of Special Collections,
University of Vermont, Burlington, Vermont.
p. 7, 8, 10, 11, 12, 13, 14, 15, 17, 18, 20, 21, 29, 30, 31, 32, 33, 34, 35, 36, 37, 38, 39

Additional credits to:

National Packard Museum, Warren, Ohio
Oldsmobile History Center, Lansing, Michigan
Shelburne Museum, Shelburne, Vermont
Smithsonian Institution, Washington, D.C.
Winton World Wide, www.geocities.com/motorcity/6064

Back cover: 1903 Winton No. 2100

Printed in the United States of America
NEWCOMB PRINT COMMUNICATIONS INC., MICHIGAN CITY, INDIANA

Related reading material:

Charles B. Shanks, "Ocean to Ocean in a Winton." *The Auto Era*, July/August 1903.

H. Nelson Jackson, "It's History Now." *Northern Vermont's Family Newspaper*,
June 24, 26, 28, 30, 1944.

Martin Sheridan, "The First Automobile Coast to Coast." *True*, June, 1952.

"First Car Across the U.S.A." *Mechanix Illustrated*, March 1953.

John S. Hammond, II, "The Whitman-Hammond Curved Dash Olds 1903 San Francisco
to Boston Expedition." *The Bulb Horn*, May-June 1978, No. 3, pp.16-23

Stephen W. Sears, "Ocean to Ocean in An Automobile Car."
American Heritage Magazine, June-July 1980.

Terry Martin, "The Transcontinental Old Pacific 2—1983—Part I." *The Packard Cormorant*,
Autumn 1984, No. 36, pp.18-33.

Terry Martin, "The Transcontinental Old Pacific 2—1983—Part II." *The Packard Cormorant*,
Winter 1984/85, No. 37, pp.14-29.

John S. Hammond II, *From Sea to Sea in 1903 In A Curved Dash Oldsmobile*.
(Egg Harbor City, New Jersey: The Laureate Press, 1985.)

Thomas F. Saal and Bernard J. Golias, *Famous But Forgotten The Story of Alexander Winton,
Automotive Pioneer and Industrialist*. (Twinsburg, Ohio: Golias Publishing, 1997.)

Curt McConnell, *Coast to Coast By Automobile: The Pioneering Trips 1899-1908*.
(Stanford, California: Stanford University Press, 2000.)

TABLE OF CONTENTS

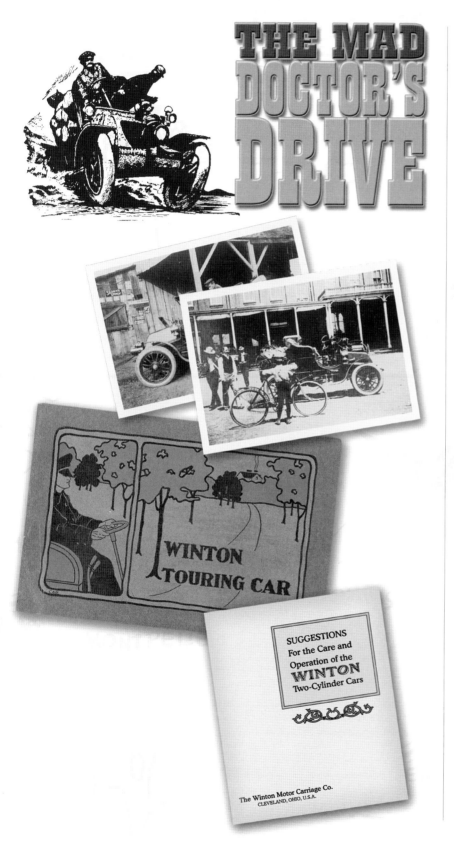

"When good roads shall be the rule, instead of the exception, in every state, it may be predicted with confidence that such journeys as that made by Dr. Jackson will be far from extraordinary. And, while the entire trip across the continent will not often be made with one machine, it is entirely within the probabilities that before a great while sturdy touring motor cars will be at the disposal of travelers for successive stages of the entire distance."

"Ocean to Ocean in a Winton"
Charles B. Shanks
The Auto Era, July-August 1903

THE MAD
DOCTOR'S
DRIVE

SAN FRANCISCO TO
NEW YORK, 1903

An account of the

1st AUTO TRIP

across the U.S.A.

as told by Ralph Nading Hill

The Mad Doctor's Drive
As told by Ralph Nading Hill

DEDICATED TO
BERTHA JACKSON KOLK

ACKNOWLEDGMENTS

The author is grateful to the Smithsonian Institution and to Mr. Don H. Berkebile, of its Division of Transportation; to Mr. Russel D. Hamilton, Greenfield, Massachusetts, and to Mr. Frank Teagle, Woodstock, Vermont; to Mr. George Daly for his drawings and Mr. Kenneth Greenleaf for his map. For generous help with the photographic illustrations appearing on pp. 12, 14, 23, 28, 32, 33, thanks are due to The Shelburne Museum, Shelburne, Vermont, and to its Staff Photographer, Mr. Einars J. Mengis. For help with the pictures, the author is also grateful to the Automobile Manufacturers Association, Inc., Dr. Otto Bettmann, Mr. James J. Bradley of the Automotive History Collection of the Detroit Public Library, Mrs. Jean Hopper of the Business, Science and Industry Department of the Free Library of Philadelphia, Miss Janet Coe Sanborn of the Cleveland Picture Collection of the Cleveland Public Library, the Science and Technology Division of the New York Public Library, Mrs. Esther M. Swift of the Vermont Free Public Library Service, and Underwood and Underwood, New York City. For her gracious help in making available the records of the late Colonel H. Nelson Jackson (who himself previously provided the author with intimate details of his journey) particular thanks go to Mrs. Bertha Jackson Kolk of Burlington, Vermont.

A part of this book appeared under the title "Six Thousand Miles in an Automobile Car" in *Contrary Country*, Rinehart and Company, New York, 1950, 1951; The Stephen Greene Press, Brattleboro, Vermont, 1961. This portion has been revised and enlarged.

Library of Congress catalog card number: 64-17559

Printed in the United States of America

FOREWORD

T he modern driver has a respectful and admiring, but rarely passionate, regard for his car. The reason, of course, is that the push-button automobiles of today are so sophisticated that they do not really *need* their drivers. That is why there are so many old car buffs and why teenagers yearn for a "stick-shift." They don't want the car to do everything for them, they want to do something for the car.

What a pity that the accident of birth a mere half-century too late denies them the fulfilment of removing a tire from a rusty clincher rim, of repairing the tube with the nutmeg grater, the patch and the glue and then, with a pinch-bar, remounting the tire and inflating it with a hand-pump to its rated pressure of one hundred pounds. Lost forever to their experience is that intoxicating ritual of taking the horse-blanket off the radiator, opening the petcock on each cylinder, squirting in raw gas with an oil can, pumping the choke a calculated number of times, and catching her on the first or second time around before the so-called self-starter gave up. No amount of chrome or horsepower can possibly compare with that heady reward of a few scattered explosions and then the steady firing that signaled the triumph of engine *and* driver over the frosty morning.

Scarcely two generations separate such enfeebling refinements as automatic choking and shifting, power steering and braking from the challenging years when no one seemed certain whether the self-starter should be powered by electricity, alcohol, ether, or a wound-up spring; whether six cylinders were six times as much trouble as one; whether a chain drive was more trustworthy than a differential, slide transmission better than planetary; whether the engine should properly be placed beneath the seat, under the bonnet, or over the rear axle; whether the doors should be on the side or the rear of a sedan, whether it should properly be labeled a fore door, fore dore, or four dour; whether there should be any doors at all on a sports car and whether it should be called a flush-sided, gunboat, or torpedo model.

The foremost problem of all—whether gas, electricity or steam was the best motive power—was reckoned by trial and error on the horsepaths, the gravel roads, and trolley tracks of America. That this required fortitude was manifest at the first annual automobile show in New York in 1900, where the steam people demonstrated that their boiler and all mountings were now placed in front of the driver, but in such a manner as not to obstruct his view ahead—the driver being seated on a transverse tank containing the feed water. They showed that the gauges, the valves, and the fire were in full view and that all operations of reversing, braking and, in short, of complete control of the vehicle were now performed from the seat.

All operations were also performed at first in the wide outdoors without benefit of top or windshield, which was just as well for the driver of the gasoline carriage, since abundant ventilation helped dispel the acrid fumes of burning oil drifting up between the floorboards. Because driving was then considered a physical and mental catharsis, the medical profession and the horseless carriage industry were joined in a faithful alliance. Cranking the engine eliminated daily calisthenics. The vibration of the roads cured insomnia. Sunlight helped anemia and the open air was good for consumption, asthma and chronic bronchitis.

Walking had its obvious merits; on a trip of any length the average driver was expected to have to do, and did do, a lot of it, as excerpts from the log of an abortive turn-of-the-century caravan pointedly testify:

Monday—

Beautiful start. Thousands saw us off. Lovely day. Roads admirable. Broke a hub at Bunkersville. Total distance for day—9 miles. . .

Thursday—

Nice weather. Road heavy. Up grade. Broke an axle. Had to send for new one to Skipperton. Made 3-1/2 miles today.

Friday—

Got early start. Covered four miles in 2 hours. Broke off buckboard. . . smashed the eccentric and lost the oil can.

Saturday—

Tinkered up the machine. Started late in afternoon. Down grade for two miles. Machine ran away. Busted everything that wasn't previously busted. Spent three hours gathering up fragments. Have covered 21-1/2 miles since Monday morning, much of it on foot.

Modern drag races, calling mostly for a heavy foot on the gas pedal, are but a mockery of by-gone cross-country and hill-climbing contests which demanded every foot-pound of energy the car could deliver and the utmost resourcefulness of its driver to gain, not just acceleration, but any movement at all. In a typical scoring system for hill-climbing, horsepower and ingenuity were bracketed as follows:

1. Very good
2. Nicely
3. Steadily
4. Well
5. Easily

6. Tacked up (one side of road to other)
7. Shed passengers to ease or help push
8. Stuck
9. Shed passengers and stuck

Among the machines at the 1903 automobile show in New York was the Winton, which has long since gone the way of the Meteor, the Moon, the Orient, the Black Crow Car and the Okey Roadster, but was then a big name in a fledgling industry. Indeed, Alexander Winton and his major rival, Elwood Haynes, were at the time engaged in a noisy controversy about who had won the most prizes and who sold the industry's first motor carriage manufactured on a regular production schedule. (A car Winton sold on March 24, 1898, now enshrined at the Smithsonian Institution, seems to merit this distinction.)

A Scotsman who had been an assistant engineer on a steamship and had labored in a New York marine engine works, Winton had gone to Cleveland in 1884 and in 1893 had begun his experiments with self-propelled vehicles. Two years later he built a motorcycle and in 1896 installed a gasoline motor in his first four-wheeled carriage. His success in establishing himself as a manufacturer seems to have been owing as much to his aggressive instinct for publicity as to his engineering acumen. When one of his early customers hitched a pair of horses to his Winton and drew it through the streets with a placard announcing "This is the only way you can drive a Winton," the manufacturer engaged a farm wagon carrying a jackass to follow it with a sign bearing the legend: "This is the only animal unable to drive a Winton."

This episode was soon forgotten in a series of well-publicized races and hill-climbing contests in which the Winton proved its mettle, and by 1903 the pioneer drivers who were taking to the roads to test themselves and their Wintons could agree with at least half of the eager Scotsman's claim that with his latest twenty-horsepower model you could "shoot over the roads or just crawl along."—R.N.H.

Bending forward to counteract wind resistance at a 1900 Chicago meet, Alexander Winton prepares to pilot his racer 50 miles in merely 1 hour, 17 minutes and 50 seconds.

The automobile was an unreliable novelty, agreed several men in the San Francisco University Club. For trips within a reasonable radius of a spare parts depot it was an uncertain means of locomotion. For longer journeys it was worthless. At this injustice being done the horseless carriage Dr. H. Nelson Jackson, a physician far from his home on the Vermont shore of Lake Champlain, felt his blood rising. It was possible, he declared, joining the group from a nearby table, to bridge the continent in an automobile. With this reckless statement the discussion suddenly became a controversy from which Dr. Jackson found he could not honorably withdraw without placing a fifty-dollar bet that he could drive an automobile across the United States.

He was fortunate that his wife did not think his age, thirty-one, too advanced for the rigors of the trip and that Sewall K. Crocker, a young mechanic from Tacoma, Washington, agreed with him that it could be done. The wager was made on May 18, 1903, and Jackson lost no time locating a Winton car which Crocker thought would have the best chance for survival. There were not very many of these in California and Jackson, a man in comfortable circumstances, paid L. C. Rowell of the Wells, Fargo & Company a handsome premium for his new 1903 Winton two-chair touring car, number 1684.

Passengers did not sit *in* this twenty-horsepower machine, but *on* it, over the two-cylinder motor, which was cranked on the right, amidships. Steering, too, was right-hand, presumably because it was more desirable to avoid the ditch than collide with an oncoming horse. But the driver or, more properly, engineer, could in any case watch the road only part of the time since the Winton boasted what was aptly called a "sight-drip oiler" that demanded constant surveillance. Fastened to the dashboard was a one-quart oil tank of brass from the bottom of which six oil pipes, each with a glass window, led to the transmission, bearings and other parts. When the oil stopped dripping the argus-eyed observer sounded an alarm and the car was halted while the pipes were unplugged or the oil supply replenished. Two long rods connected to petcocks on the cylinders served to relieve pressure while cranking, a foot-plunger controlled the air-intake valves, hence the speed of the motor; there were two levers for shifting and a third to advance or retard the spark, and a rod to the muffler cut-out to afford more power during a hard climb. The manufacturer had thoughtfully provided a tilting steering wheel that enabled a portly driver to squeeze into his seat.

West end of eastbound Winton before part of the load vanished among the ruts and bumps of deteriorating roads.

With no less care than a quartermaster equipping an infantry platoon for the field, Jackson and Crocker, who had signed up for the trip, selected their equipment and accessories: waterproof sleeping bags with blankets, rubber mackintoshes, leather coats for cold weather, corduroy suits and canvas outer suits, two tin canteens and a canvas bag of water, a fireman's ax and shovel, a telescope, a rifle, shotgun and two automatic pistols (for protection against outlaws and to secure game for food in sparsely populated areas), fishing rods, a set of machinists' tools and spare parts, a vice and pair of jack screws, and a block and tackle. The bonnet housed the radiator, the water supply and a twelve-gallon tank of gasoline. Twenty more gallons were strapped on behind and room was somehow found for an extra five gallons of cylinder oil for the drip system. The two spare tires strapped to the front of the bonnet lent the car the appearance of going when it was coming. With Jackson a six-footer scaling over two hundred pounds, Crocker, one hundred fifty and the accessories several hundred, the total weight of the expedition came to more than a ton and a half.

Cheerfully accepting the estimated time for the trip at between six weeks and six months, Mrs. Jackson took the train for the East. At one p.m. on Saturday, May 23, only five days after the wager was made, the two pioneers were off—the four-cycle engine under the seat firing with reassuring regularity; the heavy two-foot flywheel flying, the cork floats in the dual carburetors floating, the ignition timer timing, the compressed-air throttle compressing and the clacking chain from the engine to the rear wheels delivering a speed of something under twenty miles an hour. Previous cross-country expeditions having ended unhappily in southern deserts, Jackson and Crocker resolved to take a northerly route, a thousand miles longer and perhaps much rougher, but far more sensible for man and machine.

Properly broken and roped, the Vermont is apparently making detour toward a water hole or the corral.

The "highway" in the dark ages before macadam and cement.

The early miles were as satisfactory as the beginning of the trip aboard the Oakland ferry, for the broad hard roads of clay and sand afforded maximum co-operation with the frail tires and busy mechanism. Because the *Vermont*, which the Winton had been christened, was encumbered by neither windshield nor top, its passengers were treated to a bouquet of poignant sights and smells as they rolled northward to Sacramento. At dusk it was apparent that even with the aid of the moon, the yellow rays of the flickering side lanterns were too feeble, and a day was spent in Sacramento securing and attaching an acetylene headlamp. Then they were off again, northwest up the Sacramento valley for two hundred miles past farming and fruit country, vineyards and mining camps.

As the menacing Sierra Nevadas loomed near, the road degenerated into ruts, bumps and "thank-you-marms," with clouds of dust enveloping the travelers in choking invisibility. Staggering and jouncing along, the *Vermont* jettisoned the cooking utensils into the road one by one. Discovering their loss Jackson and Crocker determined that living off the countryside or starving was less to be feared than a return trip. Soon they were chugging along over adobe clay, which was satisfactory when dry but when wet quickly accumulated on the spokes of the wheels and mudguards and brought the car to a standstill. Attempting to navigate one of the earliest of many bridgeless streams they splashed into the fordway and stalled in the middle. Anchoring the block and tackle to a tree

on the far bank they slowly hauled the mud-caked Winton from its mountain bath. The rocky ascent and descent of the mountains became the most harrowing part of the journey. The "road," chipped from the cliff, often narrowed to a mere ten feet and was strewn with boulders which had to be removed by hand. Meeting a wagon on this benchway required backing as much as a mile to a place where the driver of the skittish horses could squeeze his wagon past.

Since the Winton's feeble brakes were no match for the steep and tortuous descent of the eastern Sierras, the travelers' teeth ground together as they swayed around hairpin turns above precipices a thousand feet high. By the time they reached Alturas, California, on May 30 their rear tires were mostly patches, and their triceps as hard as flint from having pumped thousands of pounds of air. Since body-building was not the objective of the expedition the Goodrich people in San Francisco were telegraphed for new rubber. After waiting in vain for two days Jackson and Crocker impatiently moved on despite the poor tires and a serious list to starboard caused by a broken front spring.

A toot from the bulb horn on the outskirts of each isolated Rocky Mountain town ended every game of roulette and Twenty-one as the inhabitants—sheepherders, traders, cowboys and staring Indians—crowded into the street to see the "devil-wagon." The novelty of the *Vermont* indeed proved as vexing as the hazards of the road. It was bad enough to have to avoid a ravine, but detours caused by human frailty were even more distressing. Already on one occasion a red-headed woman on a white horse had sent Jackson and Crocker fifty-four miles out of their way, as it turned out, in order to pass her house so that her family could see an automobile. Some of the natives of the hinterlands had never heard of a car. They thought the Winton was a small railroad engine that had somehow strayed off the track and was following the horsepaths.

The transcontinentalists measured their progress not in miles but in rods until the new tires caught up with them. There was so much scar tissue on one of the old ones that they had abandoned it and run on the burlap in which the spares had been wrapped. Gasoline was usually available in

the villages but the price (those many years before taxes and inflation) was never less than thirty-five cents a gallon and there was no ceiling. On one occasion Jackson had to pay $5.25 for a five-gallon tin of gas. (He later learned, somewhat unhappily, that the man responsible for this holdup was a native Vermonter.) Only once, near Silver Springs, Oregon, did the supply of this vital fluid become exhausted. Almost as if they were standing on the gallows waiting for the trap door to drop, Jackson and Crocker listened as the final medicine-dropperful of gas filtered through the car-

Flayed rubber on fragile 32-by-4-inch clincher tires is cooled in one of the many bridgeless mountain brooks.

buretors. The *Vermont* fired irregularly a few times, belched, wheezed and was still. The sounds of the forest now replaced the turmoil of the motor. Here, clearly, was a chance for leg work. The durable Crocker obliged with a twenty-nine-mile all-night trek to the nearest settlement, returning in the morning with ten gallons of gas and three of benzine.

Slowly and unsteadily the *Vermont* negotiated the Rockies, pulsing forward through the mists of early morning, through yellow patches of afternoon sun and the deep shadows of twilight; through mountain windstorms and slanting rains, through gullies of red clay, over lava beds of extinct volcanos and between the boulders of dried-up creeks. A twelve-hour day over such unwilling terrain left scarcely an ounce of energy in either driver, and they preferred sleep-laden mountain nights to those passed in the towns amid all-night whooping, tumult and gunfire.

It was at Caldwell, Idaho, that Bud, the third member of the expedition, was added. There was not enough room on the car for a Great Dane, a collie or even an Airedale—there was enough for a bulldog, and Bud was of that hardy variety. He came trotting up while the drivers were examining their tired motor and shortly made it clear that he belonged to no one, had no particular destination in mind, and wanted to cast his lot with them. After a few miles he became a sea-

Thrill on the prairie: gallant Crocker offers a joyride in the latest thing in transport.

Drawing crowds at a typical stop are the Vermont with (l.-r.) Jackson, Crocker and the ever-faithful Bud.
(Photo courtesy of Smithsonian Institution—Washington, D.C.)

One of numerous menacing "buffalo wallows" calling for the ultimate weapon: the indispensable horse.

soned passenger, sharing in all the excitement of the road. At first sudden jolts brought his jaw into contact with the cowling and his teeth together with an audible clack. Soon he was eyeing the road for obstructions as intently as his masters and, as the front wheels approached a rock, rut or ditch, he would brace himself skillfully in preparation for the shock. The roughness of Idaho roads fully taxed his ingenuity. The moment the car stopped he would jump down on the road and fall into a deep sleep.

Before the *Vermont* had crossed Idaho the "cyclometer" fell off, so that the three adventurers no longer knew how fast they were going or how far they had come. Jackson engaged a cowboy to pilot them across the endless plains. Near Mountain Home the worst mudhole of the journey trapped the *Vermont*, the wheels sinking into what appeared to be a mixture of mud and quicksand. Finding himself suddenly adrift the dog paddled for the bank while Jackson and Crocker hurriedly removed everything that could be dismantled. If there had been a tree the block and tackle would have solved the problem in the usual manner, but there was nothing to which it could be fastened. Presently the weary motorists located a strong branch which they succeeded in anchoring in a posthole dug on the far bank. The tackle was attached and the engine, now scarcely above the surface of the water, was started. With the working end of the tackle fastened to the rear axle which acted as a windlass, the *Vermont* customarily wound itself out of a mudhole; but this time it would not budge. Jackson and Crocker spent four unavailing hours in the water. A four-horse team finally dislodged the saturated machine from what the travelers henceforth termed their "twenty-four-horse-power mudhole," and the journey was resumed.

Crossing into Wyoming the *Vermont* encountered a wasteland of sand and sagebrush which presented almost insuperable difficulties. Even with ropes wound about them the wheels shuddered helplessly in the loose sand. Adopting the only conceivable measure, Jackson and Crocker cut bundles of sagebrush and laid them down in front of the car for a hundred feet. As soon as they had driven this distance they gathered up the sagebrush and repeated the process until the worst of the area had been crossed. They thought they were in the vicinity of the Green River and rejoiced when they at last reached the stream, only to continue for thirty-six hours among the grotesque badlands of this desolate terrain without food or sight of any living creature. Tightening their belts the famished transcontinentalists began to imagine a meal of roast bulldog and as the hours passed they stole speculative glances at Bud. Fortunately they came upon a lone sheepherder who cooked them some mutton stew. He would not take a cent, although Jackson would have given him a hundred dollars if he had asked for it. He finally presented him his rifle. As for Bud, he had handily

Progress with the original two-cylinder sod-buster is made at mole's pace in inches, feet and yards.

survived the long fast. A Wyoming newspaper referred to him as a "tortoise-shell bulldog whose eyes are badly bloodshot from exposure to alkali dust. It is to be doubted if he is enjoying the journey as he spends most of his time resting under the car." Bud's lot was improved when Jackson bought him a pair of goggles. Shortly the dog refused to start out in the morning until his glasses were put on.

Navigated only by compass, the *Vermont* jolted on, plagued by the hazards of alkali faults, boulders and, one day, as many mudholes as miles traveled. Bridgeless streams and gullies often were shallow with firm beds of pebbles affording easy passage. Occasionally the drivers were able to cross on railroad bridges, bumping over the ties between trains, but most of the time they had to block-and-tackle across, an operation that was repeated seventeen times on one particular day as they struggled to reach the Continental Divide. The *Vermont* also foundered regularly in what the natives called "buffalo holes or wallows." At one point a bargain was struck with a group of heavily laden Italian immigrants on foot—the *Vermont* to carry their belongings to the next town in exchange for their muscle-power at intervening buffalo wallows. Because of the merciless pounding the aging parts were being subjected to, the threat of mechanical failure hung over their heads like the Sword of Damocles. In Montpelier, Idaho, the ball bearings rolled out of one of the front wheels, immobilizing the car for a day while Crocker made repairs with some bearings he had taken out of a mowing machine. These were kept in place by a new cone of steel tempered by Crocker and tooled by a machinist at a Diamondville, Wyoming, coal mine. In Rawlins, on the way from the livery stable to the hotel, a stud bolt let go and the connecting rod pierced the crankcase. Five days were consumed waiting for parts from the Winton factory in Cleveland.

*In sagebrush country:
the Mad Doctor at the wheel…*

*…madder Doctor in
equally familiar attitude.*

Between Rawlins and Laramie the travelers felt the full impact of terrain that had never been adjusted to travel by horseless carriage. Near Medicine Bow crossing, for three miles beyond Rattlesnake Canyon and Elk Mountain, the natives were using the highway as an irrigation ditch. Cruising successfully through this, the two men now faced the Laramie range, the last obstacle before the great upsweep of the Rockies had been conquered. Beyond the Continental Divide there would at least be fewer occasions when they would have to hoist the *Vermont* over the crest of some craggy ascent by block and tackle. Fortunately their sturdy machine rose to the challenge and they were soon in Cheyenne on the edge of the charitable, if endless, Great Plains.

The enthusiasm of the press and the excitement of the people mounted with brightening prospects for completion of the trip. An old Wyoming native asked Jackson where he had come from. When told San Francisco, he asked where to, receiving the reply, New York.

"Automobilists" and Winton flaunt cross-country mud as a badge of achievement to foil their detractors.

"Where is your home?" was the next question. When he was told Vermont, the old man said: "What in *Hell* will you Vermonters do next?" In Nebraska a farmer saw the muddy Winton chugging toward him carrying its muddy drivers and dog, all wearing goggles. Cutting loose his horse the terrified Nebraskan seized his wife and dived under his wagon. Another farmer wanted to know "how long the derned thing would run after she was wound up?" One boy rode a horse sixty-eight miles to see the *Vermont*. Asked if he had ever seen a car he replied, "I have seen lots of pictures of 'em but this is the first real live one I ever saw."

Except for sudden prairie thunderstorms with no possibility of seeking cover, and a plague of grasshoppers so thick that the wheels could gain no purchase, the trip along the old Nebraska military highway and stage route was rapid and unmarked by crippling delays. Just west of Omaha the front axle snapped but the ingenious Crocker secured an iron pipe and fitted the broken ends of the axle into it. The Winton literally dashed from Omaha to Chicago in two days. The newspapers heralded the completion of each leg of the journey with headlines such as FROM OCEAN TO OCEAN IN AN AUTOMOBILE CAR, or "BEE-LISTS" STOP HERE. Receptions were given by city officials and automobile dealers. In every town crowds gathered to press Crocker and the "mad doctor" with questions, while the village wits indulged in jests that the travelers had already heard dozens of times. Even the dog, it was said, howled with dismay every time he heard the hoary "auto-mow-hay" joke.

The Winton Motor Carriage Company in Cleveland was transported about all the

Respite for a hot Winton winching herself up a riverbank.

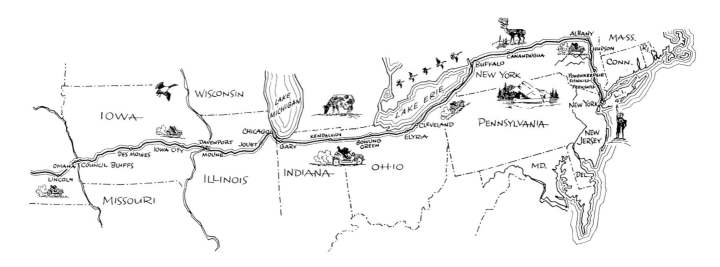

free publicity. In the absence of Alexander Winton who was in Europe, Charles B. Shanks, an executive of the company, assembled a party of well-wishers and motored to Elyria in a cavalcade of new rear-entrance Wintons to greet the transcontinentalists. They were then escorted to a Cleveland hotel for a testimonial banquet, while the dog, showing his teeth, held inquisitive newspapermen and mechanics at a respectful distance from his car. The Winton people wished to replace the front axle, overhaul and clean the haggard machine, but Jackson wanted no aid from the factory that would brand his tour as a promotional stunt. He insisted that representative mud from every state along their route from California should remain on the vehicle until the towers of Manhattan were sighted. There was good reason for this. Already in some quarters the adventurers were being called agents of the Winton company. They were said to have traded cars, as an equestrian changes his mount. They were accused of having put the *Vermont* on a train and thus covered some of the distance by rail. Subsequently the Winton Motor Carriage Company offered $10,000 to anyone who could prove these allegations. Jackson added $15,000 to the award, but the handsome sum went unclaimed. Meanwhile other motorists groomed their machines and started out across the Rockies in the hope of eclipsing the time being established by the pioneers.

With another range of mountains, the Alleghenies, in their path, Jackson and Crocker elected to favor the *Vermont* with the longer water-level route through Buffalo and Rochester. A choice of the former alternative, however, might have prevented the only real accident of the trip, which occurred east of Buffalo. At a speed of some twenty miles an hour the car struck a hidden obstruction and vaulted into the air, throwing out both the drivers and the dog and tearing off the mudguards. Since examination revealed that various bones, human and canine, were intact and the motor was still running, the trip was resumed. In Rochester the tired and dusty veterans of Redbluff, Beaver, Winter Canyon and Pit River Falls, of Silver Springs, Mountain Home, Bitter Creek and Medicine Bow were asked by a policeman what kind of cough syrup they were selling.

At length they approached the Hudson. As they flew southward along its banks (they covered the last 230 miles in 24 hours) the night editors of New York papers charted their progress, hoping that

Men, dog and car
rejoice on firm
Chicago pavement.

the morning edition of July 26 could carry news of their arrival. A correspondent from *Automobile Topics* and an eastern agent of the Winton Company drove Mrs. Jackson north to greet her husband en route. They intercepted the adventurers in Fishkill, and the "mad doctor" embraced his wife in happy reunion. As it was nearly midnight the journey was resumed at once. In Peekskill the *Vermont* suffered one final, maddening puncture. The management of the Raleigh Hotel kindly kept their outside light burning until the patch could be glued on. A leaky tire valve delayed the motorists once more in the woods a little further south. As was his custom Bud jumped down the moment the car stopped and stretched out on the road in deep slumber. As Crocker adjusted the valve in the semidarkness, hoot owls broke the silence of the woods, and a passing Albany steamer momentarily flashed its searchlight on the solitary workers. When the motors of the two cars were started again, Bud sleepily jumped into the wrong car. Jackson called out to him sharply. The correspondent for *Automobile Topics* reported that "the dog, hearing his master's voice, looked up

Three Wintons meet in Ohio
as two sporty rear-entrance
models welcome the travel-worn
veteran from the West.

sharply, then turned lazily to gaze up into the faces of the men on the car in which he was riding. Half dazed, like a man aroused from a deep sleep, the poor animal seemed at a loss to understand when the transfer had been made or how it happened that there were two cars, he in one and his owner in the other."

At half past four, when the *Vermont* crossed the Harlem River, the correspondent affixed a number of American flags to the battle-scarred machine. Fifth Avenue was asleep as the historic trip across the continent ended at the Holland House. "A mud-becoated automobile," reported the

Goggles are abandoned as proud trio roll through tranquil countryside on final leg of epic expedition.

New York *Sun*, "found a haven of rest in an uptown storage station last night after the longest motor vehicle journey on record."

Jackson and Crocker had traveled six thousand miles in sixty-three days, having spent nearly three weeks of this period repairing, resting or waiting for spare parts. Alexander Winton, brightening from the discouragement of the Gordon Bennett race in which his car had not fared well, telegraphed from Europe: "It is now up to me to design cars which shall equal if not excel the great record made by Dr. Jackson and Mr. Crocker." Barney Oldfield, to whom the public was comparing Jackson for enterprise and daring, considered the trip an outstanding accomplishment and the Winton a great car.

After a short rest, Jackson, Crocker and Bud started north, Mrs. Jackson proceeding to Vermont by train. Near Albany the high-speed gear disintegrated, causing a twelve-hour delay. In Shelburne, Vermont, only a few miles from home, the breaker box broke. Crocker made a new one out of old parts, and it was soon the privilege of the *Vermont* to tow Jackson's brothers' welcoming vehicle, which had blown out a cylinder head, into Burlington. The invincible *Vermont* suffered a final mishap just as the doctor was driving it into his carriage house. After serving valiantly all the way across the wide country, the clacking chain to the rear wheel snapped in two.

But the epilogue was written in a news dispatch dated October 3, 1903: "Dr. H. Nelson Jackson, first man to cross the continent in an automobile, was arrested in Burlington, Vermont, and fined for driving the machine more than six miles an hour."

FROM
SAN FRANCISCO
IN A
WINTON

THE recent triumph of our standard, regular model 20-horse power Touring Car is without parallel in American automobile history. When Dr. H. Nelson Jackson, of Vermont, who was spending the season in California, decided to attempt the transcontinental trip, he consulted neither manufacturer or sales agent, but purchased a second-hand Winton Touring Car at a premium price, and after three days preparation bid farewell to friends in San Francisco and started upon the long ride toward New York City.

At the time of starting the main route over the Sierras which follows the line of the Southern Pacific Railway was congested with snow and closed to all traffic. It was necessary, therefore, to make a long detour north into Oregon to find a passable trail across the high ranges. The route necessitated crossing the Great Desert where the disheartening difficulties of sand, alkali and sage brush wastes were battled with and mastered. This route led far away from railroads and possible bases of supply, but the plucky tourists plunged into the open country and "took chances." The thrilling experiences in that remote and desolate country, as recited by Dr. Jackson and Mr. Croker, his traveling companion, contribute a most interesting chapter to the world's history of automobile touring.

THE WINTON MOTOR

FACTORY
CLEVELAND

TO
NEW YORK CITY
IN A
WINTON

IT was not a specially constructed car with attachments designed for special service in the mountains and upon the deserts. The men who occupied the seats were not selected factory mechanics who had spent weeks and months in preparation. There was no elaborate system of relays for duplicate parts, new tires and general supplies. Dr. Jackson started out with one extra tire, four extra spark plugs, a shovel, an axe, a block and tackle, a cooking and camp outfit and a bulldog. When he came " out of the west" he narrated the interesting facts of his remarkable journey—he told his own story in a modest way, there having been no paid advertising agent in the party whose duty it was to disseminate fiction.

Dr. Jackson kept a detailed and accurate record of this, the first successful ocean to ocean automobile journey. It is interesting to read. He has kindly consented to its publication and those who care to have it may obtain a copy of this illustrated record by addressing the Winton Motor Carriage Co. Ask for " The Transcontinental Automobile Record." (It will be published in the forthcoming number of the Auto Era.)

ARRIAGE COMPANY,
O OFFICE:
OHIO, U.S.A.

TECHNICAL NOTES

The car in which H. Nelson Jackson and Sewall K. Crocker made their historic trip is now on view in the Museum of History and Technology at the Smithsonian Institution in Washington, D.C., the gift of Jackson in 1944. In the catalog of the Smithsonian automobile and motorcycle collection (Bulletin 213), Smith Hempstone Oliver describes it as follows:

The water-cooled engine is of the 2-cylinder, 4-cycle, horizontal-opposed type located near the center of the frame, beneath the left seat. The bore is 5-1/4 inches, and the stroke 6 inches. The flywheel is located in about the center of the vehicle; it rotated in a vertical plane parallel with the sides of the frame. It is 24 inches in diameter, with a rim 2-1/2 inches thick and 3-1/2 inches wide. The engine is suspended in place from two chassis cross members.

Each cylinder is fitted with a carburetor, one of the earliest instances of multiple carburetion on a standard-production machine. An exhaust pipe leads from each cylinder to a common muffler, the latter equipped with a cut-out operated by a small lever in front of the driver's seat. On the left side of the engine is an enclosed train of gears which drives the two exhaust camshafts, the water pump, and the ignition timer. The timing-gear cover is of aluminum.

The water system includes the water jackets on the two cylinders, the centrifugal pump of aluminum, a radiator, and a water-storage tank, together with the necessary piping. The radiator, composed of horizontal tubing fitted with radiating disks, is placed in the front of the car and behind an opening in the wooden hood fitted to the body at the front.

Behind the radiator is a cylindrical tank made of two separate sections, the left one for water. A filler cap is provided at the top of the tank, while an overflow pipe is located within the tank. A pipe from the water jackets at the top of the engine cylinders leads to the bottom of the radiator. The top of the radiator is connected to the side of the water tank, while a pipe connects the bottom of the tank to the pump, the case of which is cast integrally with the water manifold at the bottom of the two cylinders.

From the bottom of the gasoline section of the tank a pipe carried the fuel to both carburetors. A shut-off valve handwheel is located on the top of the tank, next to the filler cap. Access to both tanks is by means of a hinged aluminum cover in the top of the wooden hood.

The carburetors, which are of rather massive construction, have float bowls equipped with cork floats. Parts of the carburetors are of aluminum, and each carburetor incorporates the intake valve for its cylinder. These valves are of the automatic, suction type and are controlled in the amount of their opening by an air-pressure system similar to that on the Winton "Bullets." An air pump, located by the rear engine cylinder, is operated by a rod connected to the skirt of the piston of the front cylinder.

When the engine was running, air was compressed, and this compressed air was supplied to the two intake valves to control the amount of their being drawn open. A foot-operated plunger and a hand valve are connected to the piping, and by opening either one the pressure was caused to drop according to the amount of opening. The lower the pressure, the more the intake valves would open, and the faster the engine would run. The carburetors contain no throttle valves.

Each cylinder of the engine has a compression release in the form of a petcock. Each petcock is operated by means of a long rod reaching to the right side of the body beneath the seat and floorboard, where the person cranking the car can easily control them. When the petcocks are closed the rods are held in the proper position by clips to prevent accidental opening.

The ignition system consists of a spark plug in each cylinder, a low-tension timer, a Jefferson spark coil, a battery, and a switch. The timer can be advanced and retarded by means of a small lever located to the right of the muffler cut-out lever.

The transmission, located to the right of the engine, and with its mainshaft in line with and connected to the engine crankshaft, is a very advanced design for its time. The housing, of aluminum, with an easily removed cover of the same material, is cubical and contains two parallel shafts. On each shaft are three wide-faced spur gears placed so that the gears on one shaft are constantly meshed with the opposite gears on the other shaft. An idler gear is interposed between the two gears of the right-hand set for reverse. The first gear on the mainshaft is free to rotate on the shaft. An extension of this gear hub, outside the housing, is integral with the driving sprocket located between the housing and the flywheel. The mating gear is pinned to the countershaft. The other two gears on the mainshaft are pinned to it, while their mating gears are free to turn on the countershaft. Each of the three gears that are free to turn is, however, fitted with a clutch in its hub, so that by clutching the proper gear a low speed, a high or direct drive, or a reverse drive can be obtained.

Two vertical clutch levers are provided at the right of the driver's seat. By pulling the left lever back, low speed is obtained by clutching the center gear of the countershaft to that shaft. By pushing the left lever forward, reverse is obtained by clutching the right gear of the countershaft to that shaft. By pulling the right lever back, direct drive is obtained by clutching the left gear of the mainshaft, and hence the driving sprocket, directly to the crankshaft extension. By pushing the right lever forward, a band brake is contracted around a brake drum attached to the driving sprocket.

A starting hand crank fits onto the right extension of the mainshaft, at the right side of the body. Oil, supplied from a sight-drip oiler on the dashboard, dripped into a set of holes in brackets within the transmission to lubricate the bushings. The gears rotated in this same lubricant. A drain plug is located in the bottom of the housing.

The frame of the car consists of angle-iron sections comprising the two side members and the front and rear cross members. Other cross members support the engine and the steering-gear housing in the frame. The steering-gear housing is of aluminum and contains a completely enclosed worm and sector. The worm is turned by a column to which is attached a steering wheel that can be tilted up to give easier access to the driver's seat. The sector is attached to a short pitman arm, which in turn is attached to the left front wheel spindle by a transverse drag link. The front axle, a solid bar, is attached to the frame by two semielliptic springs, one at each side. Full shackles are used only at the rear ends of these two springs. Spindles attached to each end of the axle are connected by a tie rod behind the axle.

The rear axle is of the tubular variety, with enclosed half-axles and exposed differential unit, the sprocket of which is driven by a chain from the driving sprocket on the output shaft of the transmission. The rear-axle assembly is externally strengthened by three truss rods. It is attached to the frame by two semielliptic springs, one on each side. Full shackles are used at each end of each spring, and two external, adjustable, radius rods are therefore fitted to the axle assembly to prevent forward and backward motion. A brake drum is attached inside each rear wheel. Contracting bands on the drums are controlled by a pedal that can be locked in the depressed position through the use of a multiple-toothed ratchet incorporated in the pedal. The pedal pivots on the front engine support and is returned to the off position by a long, narrow coil spring.

WINTON TWO-SEAT TOURING CAR NO. 1684

The historic Winton as it was when Dr. Jackson gave it to the Smithsonian (above) and after its restoration (below).

The four wheels are of the wooden-spoked type with nondemountable rims. Fitted to the rims are 32-by-4-inch clincher tires. New inner tubes, contributed by Harvey S. Firestone, Jr., in May 1954, allow the ancient tires to remain inflated. The wheelbase of the car is 91 inches and the tread 56 inches.

The sight-drip oiler consists of a horizontal, cylindrical, brass tank secured to the dashboard in front of the driver; it is capable of holding about one quart of oil. Six oil lines, each incorporating a small sight glass, lead from the bottom of the tank. At the top of the tank are six adjustable valves that enable the flow of oil to be metered or shut off. The first and third lines from the right lead into the transmission, while the fifth and sixth lead to the main bearings of the engine. The second and fourth are now disconnected, though the fourth probably led to the air pump.

$25,000 REWARD!!!

LAST week we offered **$10,000.00** to anyone who could produce the slightest evidence showing the truth in any of the various malicious stories told by the "anvil chorus" about Dr. H. Nelson Jackson and his successful transcontinental ride with a Winton Touring Car. To date no one has appeared to claim the reward. The attacks upon Dr. Jackson's honor have pleased him no more than they have us, and he has authorized us to add **$15,000** to our original reward, so we raise the amount and now offer

TWENTY-FIVE THOUSAND DOLLARS

This amount we will pay to anyone proving that at any time on his journey across the Continent conditions of transportation were other than represented by Dr. Jackson.

Dr. Jackson's great triumph with his regular model Winton is a bit discomfiting to some others interested in transcontinental "stunts," especially when it is considered that he is not a mechanic, nor was he accompanied by a factory mechanic, or met at frequent intervals *en route* by factory mechanics with parts and supplies of all kinds. But the fact remains that aside from showing himself a clever amateur sportsman and a good automobilist, he demonstrated beyond question that the Winton Touring Car is the best automobile for long-distance touring manufactured or sold in America.

Send for Booklet illustrating and describing the first successful Ocean-to-Ocean automobile ride

THE WINTON MOTOR CARRIAGE CO.

FACTORY AND HEAD OFFICE:

CLEVELAND, Ohio, U. S. A.

Starting rumors that Jackson's trip was a hoax, Winton's rivals groomed their own machines and drivers for similar expeditions in the hope of achieving better time and performance, but no one ever claimed the reward.

The 2-seated body is of wood, with upholstery of tufted black leather. The two side step plates are of iron, while the four laminated fenders and the removable hood are wooden. Side lamps, a single head lamp, and a bulb horn were originally fitted but are no longer part of the equipment. A spare tire is attached to the left side of the body, though on the famous trip the spare was carried over the front of the hood. None of the five tires are original, nor were they used on any part of the trip. In the tonneau of the car, covered with a tarpaulin, is much of the spare equipment and tools that were carried on the trip.

THE END

The Mad Doctor's Drive by
Ralph Nading Hill

Winton
1903

The Picture Album

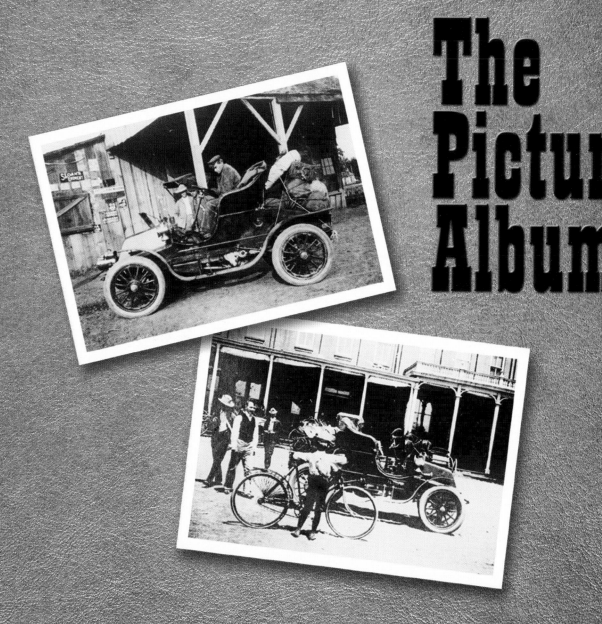

Additional photographs & illustrations relating to the 1903 drive from San Francisco to New York City

THE WEEKLY HERALD

MONDAY, JULY 20, 1903.   PRICE TWO CENTS.

MAKES BRIEF REST HERE

Dr. Jackson Stops In LaPorte on Cross Country Auto Drive

TO NEW ENGLAND FROM PACIFIC COAST

Mountains and Deserts Are Crossed—Machine Frequently Hoisted From Mud of Roads—Minneapolis Men on Their Way to Cleveland Stop In LaPorte.

Two touring cars on unusually long drives have been in LaPorte within the past 48 hours, one enroute from San Francisco to Burlington, Vt., and the other enroute from Minneapolis, Minn., to Cleveland, O.

Dr. Nelson Jackson of Burlington, Vt., accompanied by his chauffeur, Sewell K. Crocker of Tacoma, Wash., reached LaPorte at 7 o'clock Saturday night, having left Chicago shortly after 12 o'clock. But a short stop was made here the tourists pushing on to South Bend, which they reached before complete darkness had set in. Much attention was attracted by the touring car owing to its having crossed the continent and the fact that the most satisfied passenger was a mascot bull dog. The start from Chicago was delayed somewhat by the disappearance of "Bud," the bull dog. "Bud" had taken it into his head to see the city and his owners and others chased him around for sometime before he could be found. The dog did not seem to mind the riding at all and was as well is (as) his master, save for slightly inflamed eyelids. The journey across the rest of the country will be made by way of Toledo, Cleveland, Buffalo, Albany, Troy, New York and from the latter city the two men will go to Burlington. When the trip is finished it is estimated they will have traveled at least 7,000 miles.

"I decided to make the trip because of a statement I overheard at the Union club of San Francisco some time ago," said Dr. Jackson in discussing his journey. "A fellow who was sitting at a table talking with others said that a trip across the country in an automobile was impossible, and had never been made. Some way or other, I became a party to the conversation, and told the gentleman that the trip was possible, but he still insisted that it was not.

"I went home with the thoughts of our conversation still fresh in my memory, and after consulting with my wife, decided to make the trip, and asked Mr. Crocker to accompany me. He thought the trip was feasible, and in four days we were eastward bound, having first laid in a camping outfit and other necessary supplies."

"Upon leaving San Francisco, we proceeded to Sacramento, and thence northward to the northern part of California. Leaving this state, we entered Oregon, traveling to the north central part of the state, passing over the Great Desert. From this point we took an easterly route, until the railroad at Ontario was met with, and, traveling through northern Idaho, we reached Blackfoot, and then Pocadello (Pocatello).

"We next struck Granger on the southern line, but shortly after leaving here we met with heavy rains and had to go sixty miles to the northward over foothills to Cheyenne. After reaching that city we followed the Union Pacific railroad, which brought us into Omaha. Here we met the toughest roads in the country, due to the heavy rains washing out the roads, and formed what are known as 'buffalo wallows.'

"The roads were so bad in this part of the country that we had to use our block and tackle 17 times in one day to rescue our machine from the mud and water, working from 5 o'clock in the morning till dark, and then we made but 16 miles. There was not a day of our trip from Granger to Omaha that this feat did not have to be performed more than once.

"When we struck the old military road in western Nebraska we met good going for the first time since leaving California, and from Omaha we followed the Great Western road into this city.

"Our adventures have been both interesting and amusing. Shortly after leaving Oregon I secured a bull dog, which we called Bud, and he has become quite a chauffeur. In fact, he watches the roads as closely as anyone, and wherever there is going to be a jump (bump) he carefully braces himself and is prepared for the bump when it comes. He was the only one that has suffered any on the trip, owing to the alkali getting into the eyes.

"For 3,000 miles we have passed over roads that have never seen an automobile. Fun we have had and plenty of it, and were looked upon as a traveling circus. Why, we would simply telephone ahead that we were coming, and the principals would close up the district schools in the villages so as to allow the children and others to see us go by. Our experiences in parts of Oregon and Idaho were laughable, for people who had never seen a railroad thought that we were part of a train that had broken loose and was running away across the country.

"About our hardest experience was in the big desert in Wyoming, when we lost our provisions and had to go three whole days without anything to eat. It was lucky for us that we finally ran across a sheep herder, who cooked us the finest meal I ever ate.

"Up to the present time I think that we have traveled about 4,000 miles. Mr. Crocker, who is with me, is but 22 years old, but is a clever chauffeur, and the success of the trip is due to his ingenuity. My car has been christened the Vermont, and is of twenty horsepower."

John H. Howard and F. E. Dickinson of Minneapolis occupied the (another) Winton motor car which reached LaPorte shortly after 9 o'clock this morning. The tourists spent last night in Valparaiso and expected to get some distance beyond Goshen before putting up for the night. They had not had much trouble since leaving Minneapolis, excepting for the giving out of tires, owing to bad roads much of the way. They expected to have fine sailing from LaPorte on through Northern Indiana.

By the time the motorists had reached LaPorte, Indiana on July 18th they gave entertaining, detailed interviews as evidenced by the article above. During the early, Western part of the trip such was not the case—"After I started I made up my mind to avoid all newspaper men, and I did not talk to one until we reached Omaha. You see my purpose was to keep the trip quiet until I was sure of success. I made this trip without any notoriety."

(Reference: Curt McConnell, *Coast To Coast By Automobile The Pioneering Trips, 1899-1908* (Stanford, California: Stanford University Press), 2000, p. 60.)

Winton loaded for the trip, but neither the auxiliary gas tank nor acetylene head-lamp have yet been attached. Photo must have been taken in San Francisco since tank is installed before leaving for Sacramento.

Sewall Crocker sits at wheel with hood open—perhaps waiting for gasoline, oil or water. Presence of like new splash shield, spare tire on the rear and no sign of Bud, the mascot, indicates an early stop, possibly somewhere in California.

Winton being admired by a boy with his bicycle. Splash shield ahead of side step support and absence of acetylene search light on the front, suggests this photo was taken upon arrival in Sacramento, California. It was there Jackson and Crocker stayed overnight and had the lamp installed.

Solar Motor Lamps
Gas   "SHOW THE WAY"   Oil

The 1903 Models of Side Lamps, Headlights, Generators and Searchlights are of the Very Latest and Most Stylish Design.

ARE THE GREATEST LIGHT PROJECTORS EVER PRODUCED

Scientifically and substantially constructed, simple, safe and satisfactory.

All our Gas Lamps are fitted with NEW PATENT VALVE which turns ON and OFF both WATER and GAS. (The Greatest Improvement in Acetylene Gas Lamps ever made).

Most Makers will make Solar Lamps their Standard Lamp Equipment

A trial will convince you, and our prices will get your business.

We want to hear from you and submit samples suitable for your car for trial and approval.

The Badger Brass Mfg. Co.
Kenosha, Wisconsin, U. S. A.

Type of gas headlight installed on the Winton in Sacramento, California. Acetylene gas is formed by dripping water on crystals of carbide. This is referred to as a self-generating lamp as gas is not supplied from a remote generator.

(Advertisement courtesy of Roger Allison—Fresno, California)

Auxiliary gas tank has a round bottom and flat top and is held in place by two iron straps to the frame. Filler neck and cap are in the center behind the search light. Petcock for draining gas into a can for transfer to main gas tank above can be seen at bottom right (car's left). Top of hood is open for cooling and/or to add gas, oil or water.

Sewall drives Dr. Jackson on first part of trip. For the first and only time it appears Jackson is wearing corrective eyeglasses (see blowup at right).

South side of *Vermont* before part of the load slipped off due to rough roads ahead. Loss occurred somewhere between Redding and Alturas, California. Splash pan between front fender and side step support appears to be bent.

No room to pass—sheep are not crossing the road but traveling along it. Early fences were built to keep cattle out of fields as well as in. Sheep dog appears to be keeping an eye on the Winton and possibly Bud as well.

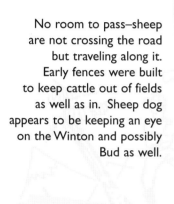

Winton negotiates a narrow trail at high altitude as evidenced by evergreens and patches of snow on the ground. Pith helmet worn by Crocker is only seen in one other photo in *The Mad Doctor's Drive*. Such helmets were also worn occasionally by Eugene I. Hammond and Lester L. Whitman of the Oldsmobile driving team a few months later.

Sewall Crocker drying off with a towel. Shadow of photographer can be seen on rear of load on Winton. Shadow on road in front of Crocker suggests another vehicle is parked alongside.

Looking out over the Winton hood along a mountain road. Note the hood is open, perhaps to aid in cooling during a climb. The leather strap to the front of the hood permits its opening and closing without the driver or passenger leaving their seats.

Dr. Jackson must have lain on the ground for this low angle photo of Sewall Crocker at the wheel. Absence of spare tire on the front suggests photo was taken during early part of the trip.

Winton appears to be stuck in soft ground and on a slight incline. From Sewall's stance it is evident he is tightening one of the clutches located under the passenger's seat while Bud contemplates his own pit stop.

Dr. Jackson pours water into radiator tank as Bud looks over his shoulder. Presence of jack under right end of front axle could explain reason for stop.

Crocker working on the engine through the opening beneath the passenger's seat. Cushion is on top of the load in back. Removal of floorboards (leaning against rear wheel) makes room for his left leg. Length of repair or speculation that this may have been an overnight stop are suggested by bed rolls in front of car, canteen on sign post and Bud sound asleep at the rear.

Sewall Crocker sorts through items on the floor of the car. Perhaps retrieving the crank before starting. Folding step with handle at the top can be seen below the frame in the rear. This was used to step into the door of rear entrance tonneau body when attached. Dr. Jackson elected to leave the heavy tonneau behind in exchange for the lighter, sloping lid.

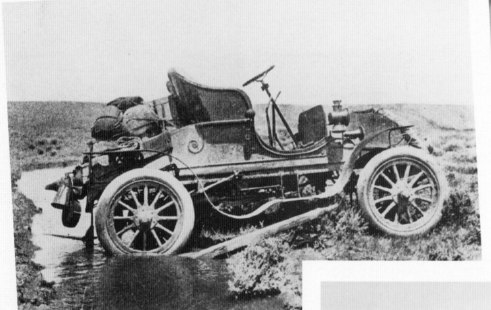

Stuck in a buffalo wallow. Hand crank is shown being held to the floor by a special clip. Photo clearly shows absence of oiler on dash.

The 1903 Winton hand crank is unique. It has an internal ratchet to disengage the handle in case the engine misfires and reverses direction. Without it the chances of a broken arm when cranking are increased a thousand fold.

(Photo courtesy of Jerry Joschko—Michigan City, Indiana)

Stuck in the mud. It appears the rear deck is being used as a plank in an effort to gain traction. It can be seen behind the car in an inverted position. The rear hubcap seems to be missing. Perhaps it was used to replace one of the front hubcaps, which are necessary to retain the front wheels and their bearings.

"Somewhere west of Laramie"–Dr. Jackson and Bud survey the road ahead. One account concerning Bud's joining the team is different from that told by Ralph N. Hill.* It relates that the residents of Caldwell, Idaho staged a dog fight between two Bull Terriers in honor of Dr. Jackson and Sewall Crocker. Dr. Jackson was upset by the spectacle but liked the winning dog. Because of this and perhaps so he wouldn't have to fight again, he bought "Bud" and made him their mascot.

*Tom Mahoney: "First Car Across the U.S.A." *Mechanix Illustrated*, March 1953.

Low angle shot by Jackson shows how spare tire is lashed to the front. Note weight of tire is carried by brackets for the search light. This also keeps the tire up so that its center provides a good flow of air through the fins of the radiator seen behind the light. Note chunks of rubber missing from right front tire. Reportedly the front tires held up for the entire trip while the rears were continually replaced beginning in Ontario, Oregon.

Winton parks at coal mine in Diamondville, Wyoming while machinist makes a new bearing cone for the front wheel.

Close up photo shows two men looking through provisions on the Winton— possibly for bearings? Note portly gentleman succeeded in upstaging the Winton in both photos taken at the coal mine.

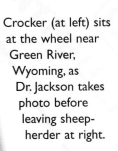

Crocker (at left) sits at the wheel near Green River, Wyoming, as Dr. Jackson takes photo before leaving sheep-herder at right.

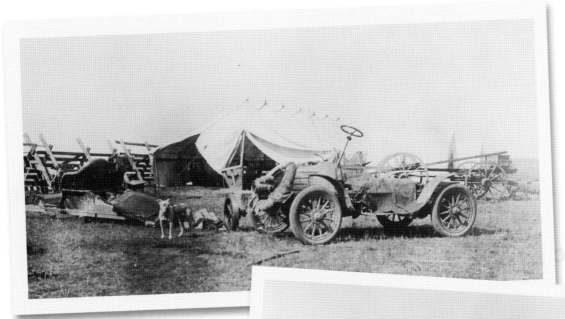

Winton disassembled to repair damage from second connecting rod failure, 18 miles east of Cheyenne, Wyoming. Work was done at a Union Pacific trackside camp. Note wooden hood and body have been removed. Aluminum radiator casting and end of water tank can be seen over the front wheel. Lattice like structure in background is a snow fence. Bud as usual is standing guard.

Jackson and Bud studying the disembodied *Vermont*. Flywheel and crankshaft can be seen by left front wheel. Crocker was able to remove the hood without untying the spare tire from the carbide headlight. Tarpaulin covers the engine while waiting for new parts to arrive from the Winton factory in Cleveland, Ohio. There is no mention of this second repair in Archer, Wyoming due to rod failure in *The Mad Doctor's Drive* by Ralph N. Hill.

The team, including Bud, stops for a photograph in Omaha, Nebraska. Just before entering town, a broken front axle had been repaired with a piece of pipe. Note (as indicated by shadow on the ground) the right rear fender has pulled away from the cast iron step plate. The fenders, made of laminated wood, are only 1/4" thick and attached to the step plates by just three bolts. The right rear fender dips down to allow clearance for cranking. The hole for the hand crank can be seen passing through the frame. The person cranking usually grabbed the fender with his left hand for support. This continual stress, plus low road clearance undoubtedly led to detachment. It was reported this fender came completely off when the car ran into a deep hole while traveling at a relatively fast pace east of Buffalo, New York.

(Photo courtesy of Smithsonian Institution—Washington, D.C.)

Bicycle mechanic poses for
Dr. Jackson's camera at the door
of his shop. Shadow reveals
effective sign hanging overhead.

Photo taken east of Buffalo, New York,
after only real accident of the trip.
Right rear fender came completely
off and the left rear is broken in half.
Photo-op taken at same location as
picture on page 18 of Hill's account.
Note goggles are on Bud and Dr.
Jackson has placed his paws on the
steering wheel. No goggles were on
Bud in photo taken minutes before.

(Photo courtesy of Smithsonian Institution—Washington, D.C.)

Crocker tips his hat to oncoming
motorists in what must be a staged
photo by Jackson. The other
automobile appears to be one
of a kind—perhaps homemade.
Note directional arrow and band
painted on telephone pole. Both
examples of early road signs.

Car on display in New York City. Note broken section of wooden rear fender is reattached.

Colonel H. Nelson Jackson sits at the wheel of his Winton before shipping it to the Smithsonian Institution in 1944. At this time the *Vermont* was 41 years old and Jackson 71. He died 11 years later. Note the broken left rear fender has been replaced. However, the original kerosene side lamps and acetylene headlight were removed.

The *Vermont* on display in the Smithsonian. The one quart, six-drip-feed oiler on the dash is not visible in any of the photos taken on the trip. Perhaps it was added after Dr. Jackson returned home.

(Photo courtesy of Peter C. Kesling Foundation — La Porte, Indiana)

(Photo courtesy of Smithsonian Institution—Washington, D.C.)

The *Vermont* after being restored by the Smithsonian. It appears to have been repainted with appropriate pin striping. The original side and headlamps are missing. Evidently, sometime after his cross-country drive, Dr. Jackson had a new, auxiliary gas tank installed under the radiator. This one has a flat bottom and the filler neck has been moved off center to facilitate filling when the acetylene headlamp is in place.

ANATOMY OF THE 1903 WINTON

1 Battery Box

2 Hole for Crank

3 Transmission

4 Flywheel

5 Low Speed and Reverse Lever

6 Hand Brake and High Speed Lever

7 Foot Brake

8 Oil Tank

9 Water and Gas Tanks
   End-to-End

10 Radiator

11 An auxiliary 12-gallon gas tank
   was mounted under the radiator
   in a space normally occupied by
   a tool drawer (not shown)

12 Steering Gear

13 Foot-controlled Air Valve

14 Compression Release
   for Easy Cranking

15 Muffler

The Two Challengers

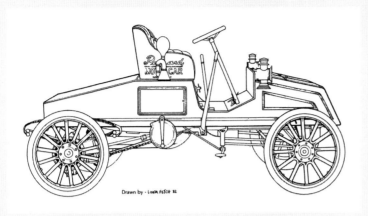

Drawn by - LINDA FETCH '92

1903 Model F Packard "Old Pacific"

(Photo from Richard Quinn Collection courtesy National Packard Museum.)

SPECIFICATIONS

ENGINE—12 Brake Horse Power, single cylinder, sheet metal jacket, geared pump, water cooled, automatic spark plug control, pedal speed regulator.

TRANSMISSION—3 direct geared speeds forward, one reverse, no idle gears in action at any time; no extra reducing gears on slow speeds; gears run in oil; any speed obtained by single motion of speed controlling lever, 1-1/2" roller chain to spur gear, differential on rear axle.

WHEEL BASE—88 inches.

TRACK—56-1/2 inches.

SPEEDS—10, 20 and 30 miles per hour

BRAKES—Band brakes on each rear wheel, worked by foot pedal. Auxillary brake on countershaft, worked by hand lever.

STEERING—Worm and segment gear.

IGNITION—Jump spark with automatic timing advance, electric fitted with special accumulator and dry batteries.

EQUIPMENT—Complete set of tools, pump, spare parts, extra oil tanks. Kerosene oil lamps. Wood wheels, 34" in diameter with anti-friction bearings, fitted with detachable double tube tires, 4" size.

Tom Fetch behind the wheel with factory machinist N.O. Allyn on the rear deck of Old Pacific somewhere in the Sierra Nevada Mountains. Until his death, Fetch insisted his car was the first to cross the country under its own power.

1903 Curved Dash Runabout "Olds' Scout"

(Photo courtesy of Oldsmobile History Center—Lansing, Michigan.)

SPECIFICATIONS

CAPACITY—Two passengers

WHEELBASE—66 inches.

TREAD—55 inches.

FRAME—Angle steel.

SPRINGS—Oldsmobile side springs.

WHEELS—28 inch wood artillery.

TIRES—3 inch detachable.

MOTOR—5 X 6 inch 7 H.P. horizontal.

TRANSMISSION—All-spur gear, two speeds forward and reverse.

FINISH—Black with red trimming.

EQUIPMENT—Complete set of tools and pair of large brass side lamps.

RADIATOR—Copper disk.

CARBURETOR—Oldsmobile.

IGNITION—Jump spark.

STEERING GEAR—Tiller.

DIFFERENTIAL—Bevel gear type.

BRAKES—Differential and rear wheel.

WATER CAPACITY—Five gallons.

CIRCULATION—Gear pump.

GASOLINE CAPACITY—Five gallons.

Lester L. Whitman (left) and Eugene I. Hammond (right) stand next to 1903 one-cylinder, five horsepower Curved Dash Oldsmobile in Boston. Dubbed the "Olds' Scout" it was modified by the factory for the cross country trip with a touring luggage box and larger radiator which can be seen hanging below the frame.

When Dr. Horatio N. Jackson left San Francisco in May of 1903, his was the only automobile headed for New York. He and his mechanic, Sewall Crocker, took their time—even stopping to fish and hunt when the occasion arose. However, by the time they reached Omaha, Nebraska there were two other autos on their tail.

The challengers were a one cylinder Packard F and a Curved Dash Olds—also powered by a one-cylinder engine. These were not "spur of the moment—it's a bet!" trips but rather well planned, financially backed promotions by their respective manufacturers. Supplies of gasoline, oil, tires and parts were readily available along the route. The Curved Dash Olds even had a factory machinist on board part of the way.

The Winton had already crossed the roughest part of the route but Jackson realized he must cover as much ground as possible each day. If another rod bearing should fail, they could be delayed for five days or more.

Ultimately, Dr. Jackson, Crocker, Bud and the Winton reached New York City on July 26th nearly a month before the Packard's arrival on August 21st. The Winton had taken 63 days to cross the country, the Packard 62. The Curved Dash Olds reached the shores of the Atlantic on September 17th after a 73-day run.

However, Tom Fetch driver of the Packard and others felt the Winton had somehow cheated its way across the Rocky Mountains. They started rumors that Jackson's trip was a hoax, the car had been placed on railroad cars part of the way and even suggested more than one car had been used by Dr. Jackson. These charges were countered by offers of $10,000 and $15,000 by the Winton Automobile Company and Dr. Jackson respectively to anyone who could prove the Winton did not make the trip under its own power. No one ever collected a cent.

However, the public's interest in crossing the country by auto was aroused and in 1904 a four cylinder, air cooled Franklin completed an amazing dash of only 33 days. In 1905 the Olds Motor Works sponsored the first transcontinental auto race between two 1904 Curved Dash Oldsmobiles. The race began in New York City on May 8th and the first Olds, "Olds' Scout," reached Portland, Oregon June 21st—just before the start of the fifth annual National Good Roads Convention. The second, "Old Steady," came in June 28th.

First Three Automobiles To Cross The United States
Between May and September of 1903

Auto	Route	Drivers	Start	Finish	Duration
Winton	————	Dr. H.N. Jackson Sewall Crocker	May 23rd	July 26th	63 Days
Packard	- - - - - -	Tom Fetch Marius Krarup	June 20th	August 21st	62 Days
Oldsmobile	••••••••••	Lester Whitman Eugene Hammond	July 6th	September 17th	73 Days

Location of All Autos on July 26th, 1903
When Dr. Jackson and the Winton reached New York City

MINIATURE WINTONS

TOY FOR CHILDREN

Early Winton by Kingsbury is made of pressed steel and 10 inches long. The strong, clockwork motor can propel it across kitchen linoleum at a relative 25 miles per hour.

The steering wheel spokes are curved as in the 1902 Wintons while the driver, with his cap and straight back, is reminiscent of Sewall Crocker himself.

SCULPTURE FOR ADULTS

The bronze sculpture, "San Francisco to New York City 1903," by Stanley Wanlass captures forever the energy and drive of both men and machine. He has recreated with detail the load of provisions on the rear deck and the feel of motion through flapping scarves, clouds of dust and unique double spoking of the wheels. Wanlass who feels the automobile is the only really new significant art form of the 20th Century is considered by many to be the finest sculptor of these machines.

Photo by Steve Tregeagle
Salt Lake City, Utah

Winton
1903
Sales Brochure

WINTON TOURING CAR

"...our system of motor government is the simplest, most effective, and gives quicker and more absolute control over the conduct of the car than any other known to automobile mechanics."

"The Winton has any number of forward speeds and there is no reaching out for levers when a change speed is desired."

"...the operator, quick as a flash, with a single forward stroke of the right arm, can disconnect the power and engage the emergency brake."

The complete and unparalleled success of the Winton double cylinder (opposed) gasoline motor demonstrates beyond cavil the entire correctness of the principles on which it was designed.

Our 1902 car with its 15-horsepower motor is the substantial foundation of the present successful model—the 20-horsepower Winton Touring Car. This latest triumph has many inherent advantages that are generously appreciated by those who recognize superiority in design and who can differentiate between practical high grade construction and superficial perfection.

To build an automobile like our present 20-horsepower model requires the work of experts. The difficult and necessarily exact construction could not be entrusted to other hands, and, as a consequence, the purchaser of a Winton secures the product of the most practical and scientific engineers and mechanics identified with the automobile building industry. Close inspection of the many pieces that combine to complete the Winton Touring Car will show that every part, large or small, bears evidence of the highest order workmanship, and we believe that in no other automobile factory can be found a more exact system for testing the quality and accuracy of every part. To bring our manufacturing system so near perfection is the result of great expense, long experience and intelligent effort.

In the development of our 20-horsepower car a new and broader opportunity was afforded our mechanicians for the display of their superior skill in the manipulation of structural materials. The first ones produced were put through a series of extraordinary tests, rigorous and prolonged, first in the factory and then over all kinds and conditions of road. At no time did the motor lag, no gradient was too severe for the car to ascend with smart speed, the new spring suspension—aided by the deep spring, upholstery of seats and high backs—yielded a degree of luxurious comfort in riding that was exceptional and altogether delightful. These severe tests proved conclusively that for speed, perfection in control, durability, economy, safety, cleanliness, and in the matter of absence of noise, vibration, and all offensive odors, the 20-horsepower Winton Touring Car was all that had been

anticipated, and indeed surpassed the expectations of its builders. It incorporates every advantage to result from strength, accessibility to all parts, ease of adjustment, long wheel base, easy steering, automatic lubrication of ample and positive character, perfect system of cooling, an absolutely reliable system of brakes, variable speed control, a perfected system of interchangeable parts, etc., etc.

This new model presents no array of complex machinery to demand the constant attention of a trained mechanic to insure satisfactory service. The motor is centrally suspended and with all centers of mass carefully and evenly distributed, there is a uniformity of responsibility upon each of the axles. When one considers the matter of tires the question of weight distribution becomes an important feature.

Motor—On brake the motor develops 20-horsepower. It is the double opposed, water cooled, standard Winton type, which experience of the most extensive and varied character has proven correct in principle. Cylinders are cast from the best grade of hard gray iron, a superior metal for gas engine construction. Top and bottom covers of crank pit are cast

aluminum. All aluminum used in Winton construction is so alloyed as to combine lightness and present exceeding strength. A great deal of this secret process alloy is used throughout Winton construction, thereby accounting for the unexcelled combination of strength and lightness.

Cranks are secure within this housing and as a consequence no oil from the motor will leak away and drip upon pavement or carriage house floors, nor is it possible for dust to work in and do injury to motor bearings. Crank case cover may be easily removed to permit a ready inspection of interior.

Connecting rods are of drop forged, open-hearth steel, with phosphor bronze bushings.

Crank shaft is forged in one piece from open-hearth steel. It is sufficiently heavy to withstand any service. The accurately proportioned crank shaft bearings are of phosphor bronze. Pistons are ground to size with microm-eter gauge and the boring of cylinders is accomplished in the same precise manner. Piston rings are cut before being turned to size, accomplished by the use of special fixtures, insuring an effective and even bearing through-out the entire circumference.

The air pump connecting rod is well secured to a lug, cast solid within the forward motor piston.

Transmission—With our improved transmission nearly all of the power generated is transmitted to the driving wheels and because of this efficiency our 20-horsepower motor is equivalent in tractive effort to many that are rated 25-horsepower or more. Builders of these over-rated motors are simply handicapped because so much power is absorbed by excessive friction in the transmission. The Winton motor saves gasoline accordingly.

Transmission gears are contained within an oil tight and dust proof case. Steel gears operate against bronze. The steel gears are cut from drop forged discs. The phosphor bearings are very carefully made and accurately proportioned.

The differential gear is of the spur type, contained within an oil tight drum. Gears are made of steel, carefully cut and very strong.

The driving chain for the 20-horsepower Winton Touring Car, compared with our 1902 chain equipment, represents a three-fold increase in strength and durability. Sides and rollers are made of best cold rolled open-hearth stock, the pins of nickel steel.

Ignition—The new ignition system possesses many features of merit. It is simple and wonderfully efficient. Everything in the circuit is protected from electrical losses due to the presence of moisture and oil. The car is equipped with two sets of batteries—one being held in reserve.

The entire absence of delicate mechanism is at once noticeable. There is but one coil used and no vibrator to bother about. The contacts on the circuit breaker both move and are self-aligning and adjusting. The type of spring used in the breaker is such as to preclude possibility of breakage. Contacts are so constructed as to give positive results. They will free themselves of any foreign deposit which, if permitted to be present, would cause trouble. The combination, taken as a whole, gives the most reliable ignition possible. A heavy glass front upon the breaker box makes it possible to observe the operation of contacts without removing box cover.

At the end of a season's service should a renewal of the contacts be necessary, it is a simple operation of a few minutes only. Unscrew the cap, insert a new plunger and it is done.

Control—Beyond the pale of argument our system of motor government is the simplest, most effective, and gives quicker and more absolute control over the conduct of the car than any other known to automobile mechanics. It is an air governor operated either by the spring button beneath the right foot or the air line valve at side of seat which is convenient to the driver's right hand. This system is as sensitive as the throttle control of a locomotive, but does not entail the annoyance of hand pumps, gauges, water glasses, etc. We have no spark regulator that requires constant shifting and reshifting, no sliding gears to be gymnastically manipulated—in fact, with the Winton system of control there need be no thought in the operator's mind other than the road ahead. One quickly learns to operate the governor foot button by instinct. A horseman driving a spirited equine will go fast or slow as he releases or increases the pressure upon the sensitive mouth through the driving reins. With the Winton control the motor speeds up and the car forges ahead when the foot button pressure is increased. Speed of car diminishes when the pressure is released. By this clever means we do not need a set of gears for every variation of speed. The Winton has any number of forward speeds and there is no reaching out for levers when a change speed is desired.

There are but two controlling levers, one operating the hill climbing and reverse gears, and the other to operate the direct driving gear and emergency brake. With this direct driving gear in action (lever drawn toward operator) any variation of speed is obtained by the pressure upon foot button. The opposite action of this direct drive gear lever (when thrown forward from its central position) is to apply a powerful emergency brake. Thus one may be driving at a high speed and in the face of sudden emergency the operator, quick as a flash, with a single forward stroke of the right arm, can disconnect the power and engage the emergency brake.

With our new 20-horsepower motor the car may be driven up all ordinary hills with the direct drive gear in action. Only on steep sand hills will the "hill climbing gear" be found necessary.

Lubrication—Transmission gears are encased and run in an oil bath. For the motor there is a reservoir beneath bonnet lid, which is connected with the float-distributing chamber by a brass tube. Float chamber is cast solid with crank pit cover. From float chamber are feed pipes connecting with the several motor bearings. The reservoir is so much higher than the float chamber that the gravity force makes a pump unnecessary. The float regulation insures an even feed of lubricant to the bearings. This system is of the most positive character and the operator's mind is free from thoughts of harm resulting to motor from improper or insufficient lubrication. Differential gears are encased and packed with solid lubricant.

Cooling—This is another feature of excellence. With our efficient centrifugal circulating pump and an ample system of radiation a minimum amount of water is required. Water is circulated so rapidly and heat radiated so effectively that the boiling point is never reached and the consequent loss is only by natural evaporation. Water pump is driven by gear and its action is positive.

Steering Gear—The improved Winton steering gear possesses every advantage. It is not rigid beyond the point of preventing shock upon the guide wheels being communicated to the steering wheel, or causing the car to deviate from its proper course. It is a development of the worm and segment principle. Steering joints are of the ball and socket type, adjusting themselves to all uneven road conditions. Steering post is of extra heavy gauge one and one-quarter-inch steel tubing. Aside from the base bearing it has a strong support in the floor of car eight inches from the base.

Steering wheel is heavy brass armed with a mahogany finished laminated wood rim. Post is hinged near the top so that the wheel may be swung forward to permit easy entrance to operator's seat.

Frame—The Winton frame of double angle and sheet steel, securely riveted, with substantial cross braces, is the staunchest possible to build. The strong iron box corner connections insure perfect rigidity to joints under all conditions of strain.

Axles—Front axle is forged solid from one piece of best axle steel. Steering heads contain phosphor bronze bushings which give bearing to the pivot

axles. Front wheels are equipped with double ball bearings. Some axles and steering heads are of handsome design, others are strong in construction, but these features in the new Winton claim the distinction of being both strong and of neat design.

The rear axle is of the tubular tri-strut type, the live axle extending through from each rear wheel to the differential gear at the center where it is secured by means of key and pin. The live axle revolves in parallel anti-friction roller bearings of our own design and manufacture.

Springs—Semi-eliptic, both front and rear. Each spring is 6 inches longer than those in 1902 construction. They are also wider, much more elastic and so attached as to prevent shifting upon the axles. Our tests with these springs have shown them to be admirably adapted for the special service required. They are very powerful and at the same time so elastic as to insure maximum comfort in riding.

Wheels—The special Winton wheel, of the artillery type, is the strongest and smartest appearing used in automobile construction. Spokes and felloes are of best grade second growth hickory. Metal hubs are of our own design.

The steel clincher rim is shrunk upon the felloe but as a means of additional security tire bolts are used at each felloe joint.

Tires—The matter of tires is an important one and the quality recommended and used by us is the best product of the tire manufacturing industry. In specifying for our tire equipment we demand, above all else, the very highest quality—price is an after consideration. The results are to our complete satisfaction, our tire being one back of which its manufacturers stand. It is of the double tube, clincher type.

Brakes—In addition to the emergency brake (see "Control") there are two others, one acting upon each drum cast solid with the rear wheel hubs. These hub band brakes are operated by a single lever convenient to the left foot. This lever works against a ratchet which permits a brake being set to hold car, forward or back, on the steepest incline.

Tanks—Gasoline, water and lubricating oil tanks are back of radiating coils beneath bonnet. All are accessible by raising bonnet lid. In their construction the best grade of heavy gauge brass is used. All joints are riveted and soldered and tank head connections are brass castings. Capacity of gasoline tank is between 11 and 12 gallons, this being sufficient to run car about 175 miles over ordinary good roads.

Muffler—The Winton muffler insures a silence in motor operation that is altogether pleasing. It is equipped with a relief slide for use on track when it is desirable to "cut out." This slide is controlled by hand from the operator's seat.

Body Construction—All lumber is air seasoned and of first quality. The ash frame mounts panels of poplar. These soft and hard woods are mortised securely with glue and screws. All outside joints are carefully avoided. The bonnet, excepting the side panels, is made of sheet aluminum. Front seat is divided, the divisions being sufficiently wide to insure comfort.

Tonneau is especially roomy and will comfortably seat three persons. Backs are very high and the top of door is flush with the top line of the tonneau. A third seat fits in the door space when door is closed. The lines of both front and tonneau seats are especially graceful and give a degree of excellence to the Winton design that is all its own.

Mud Guards—Continuous mud guards are introduced with this model. They are made of laminated wood of a quality possessing unusual strength and toughness. Each guard is made in two sections, the sections joining at the side step to which they are secured.

Finish—Standard coloring combines a light maroon body and glazed carmine running gear, both artistically striped. Mud guards are finished in black with carmine striping. So thorough is our process that three weeks are required for work to go through the paint and varnish departments, during which time the body undergoes twenty-seven operations.

With our new model just enough polished brass is used in the finish to enliven the general effect. A quarter inch half round brass molding follows the top outside lines of front seats and tonneau, a half inch half round brass molding is mounted on the bonnet board, the handles of the controlling levers are brass, steering wheel is brass armed, grips and locks upon tonneau door and bonnet are of solid brass, also the hexagon acorn nuts which secure bonnet to frame. This touch of bright metal here and there, together with the full brass lamps, hub caps and horn, produce an effect which is pleasing to the eye.

Upholstery—In this department, as in all others throughout the Winton factory, only expert workmen are given opportunity to show their cleverness and skill in the manipulation of the most expensive materials. Cushion springs are of oil-tempered spiral, the curled hair is the best, and all leathers used are hand buffed and highest grade. Every detail combines to yield luxury. In the matter of comfort nothing could be more satisfactory than are the seats and backs of this new car.

Lamps—The regular lamp equipment consists of two full brass oil lamps of best manufacture and quality. They attach to each side of bonnet board.

Start Motor—This requires only a few seconds, for there are no fires to start or delays of any sort. Turn on the battery switch and with one revolution of the starting crank the motor is set in motion. This requires the same small amount of time and energy whether motor has been inoperative ten minutes or ten days. The Winton is always ready to start and go. To stop the motor the switch is turned off.

PRICE	TERMS
The twenty horse-power Winton Touring Car as herein described, complete with detachable tonneau, two full brass side lamps, tools, horn, etc., the price is $2,500.	Net Cash, f.o.b. Cleveland. Twenty percent of purchase price to accompany order, balance on delivery to transportation company. Orders are executed in rotation.

Winton
1903

The Instruction Manual

SUGGESTIONS
For the Care and
Operation of the
WINTON
Two-Cylinder Cars

The Winton Motor Carriage Co.
CLEVELAND, OHIO, U.S.A.

"Maintain a cool head at all times, and master the interesting details of operation before venturing near brick walls and telegraph poles."

REMEMBER

That an automobile has no brains.

You must do its thinking.

It is merely a man-made machine,

subject to man's control, and under

thoughtful handling, will perform all the

work for which it is designed.

Original, Owner's Instruction Manual
Courtesy of Robert Stormont—Rockford, Illinois

WINTON
Two-Cylinder Cars

Study the following instructions carefully, and know "where you are at" before attempting to start motor or operate car.

To Start Motor.—The mechanical spark advance lever (B-17) must be shoved down to the lowest point below the notches before inserting ratchet crank handle for starting motor, otherwise crank cannot enter. Open the air line by unturning the valve (A-12) next to spark advancer; turn on electric switch (A-11) and with crank turn motor over. When motor starts remove crank, immediately advance the spark lever to the first notch, then close the air line (A-12). When operation of carriage begins, advance or retard the spark as the speed of motor and other conditions warrant.

The double wheel valve* below cushion seat (A-10) is an adjustment, operating on the air line, to regulate what is termed the "governor," or minimum speed of motor when carriage is at rest. The four armed wheel acts as a lock nut. After the proper adjustment has been obtained by regulating the center wheel, secure the adjustment with this lock nut attachment.

(*1903 and 1904 models have a small adjustable valve on right side of body under driver's seat. The adjustment for maintaining proper governor speed is made by loosening the small set screw and turning segment or stopper on inside of body under driver's seat one way or the other. Set this valve so marker points to "Open" when starting motor.)

1

Before starting the motor *be sure that gasoline and lubricating oil are turned on* at main supply valves over tanks.

One feature in connection with starting motor, which should be the subject of caution, is *the avoidance of passing over point of highest compression when starting crank is on its downward stroke*. Pull up on crank slowly until the effort is met by some of the compression resistance, then lower the crank one or two ratchet notches and, with a firm arm, pull up on the crank rapidly and without hesitation turn pistons over the compression center. By so doing there is no possibility of shock resulting to the wrist.

Should the motor evidence any disinclination to start at first turning of crank, investigate the valves (B-20), which regulate the gasoline supply to carburetors. If there is any possibility of there having been a too great quantity of fluid admitted, shut off the supply from each carburetor and work the surplus out. To accomplish this more easily open the cylinder relief cocks and continue turning motor.

There is a one-sixteenth inch hole drilled in the bottom of each carburetor, placed there to prevent flooding. Keep these holes free from obstruction. Should the failure to start not be due to gasoline supply, investigate the spark. Remove cover from breaker-box (B-15) on left side of motor, clean contact points (B-22) carefully, and see that when cam (B-14) trips spring, these points come firm in contact. If contact is not firm, correct the difficulty by turning down the adjusting screw (B-18).

Remove the spark plugs (A-4 and 19) occasionally, and if coated

2

with carbon clean them carefully, removing all carbon deposit. An old tooth brush, a piece of cloth or waste may be used in cleaning.

If there is an absence of explosion, due to causes other than gasoline feed or contact of points in breaker-box, switch on the reserve set of batteries, and it may be found that this will give the desired result. Be careful at all times that the wiring is secure at all connection points. See that binding screws on spark coil box are at all times secure. Keep the battery cells (A-7 and 8) dry, and avoid, as much as possible, getting lubricating oil upon any of the insulation throughout. Keep contact points (B-22) clean. If they are oil covered, wipe them with cloth before starting motor.

On long runs it is desirable to rest the batteries by occasionally shifting from one set to the other, thereby giving the alternate one a chance to recuperate. The switch for this is attached to front of battery box (A-9).

It is possible that when you receive Car from the transportation company, and for the first time open the main gasoline admission valve above the tank, the gasoline will flood the carburetor float-box. Such a condition would manifest itself by fluid escaping through the small vent tube on top of float-box. In such case the float within the box has tightened a little and it may be readily loosened by striking a few easy blows upon side of float-box with a wrench or any other light tool. See that floats are working properly before carburetor valves are opened.

After mastering the details of starting motor, the operation of sparking device, carburetor admission valves, etc., it is next in

3

order to learn the operation of the transmission gear and the driving of Car.

When motor has been started, occupy seat behind steering wheel. The right foot is then convenient to the foot or "governor," button (A-21), and the left foot is free to operate the brake. Put an easy pressure upon the governor-button and the motor speed will increase. Take hold of the short inside lever and draw it gradually into place until it notches. This engages the low speed gear, and the effect is to propel the Car forward. To stop Car, first remove foot from button and then release the short lever to its CENTRAL position and apply the brake. To stop motor, turn electric switch button to register "OFF."

This same short lever, when shoved forward from its CENTRAL position, engages the reverse gear. To run Car backward, engage this reverse gear.

After having become thoroughly familiar with the short lever-forward and backward control—learn the manipulation of the long outside lever. Start Car ahead by using the short lever, then, after releasing the short lever to its CENTRAL position, gradually draw in the long lever, which will engage the high-speed gear clutches. When high-speed gear is engaged it is possible to obtain any variation of the Car speed, from maximum to minimum, by the manipulation of the governor-button.

By the intelligent operation of this governor-button it will quickly be observed that the Car can be made to spurt ahead or slow down, as the will of the operator may elect. Consequently there is no necessity for juggling the levers in controlling the speed of Car.

4

In taking corners, for instance, do not diminish Car speed by throwing out the clutches, but do it all with the governor-button control.

To regulate Car speed by governor-button, rather than by clutch operation, insures economy of fuel and power, and does not permit motor to race.

To stop Car, disengage the high-speed gear clutch by shoving long lever forward and apply brake, as hereinbefore explained.

When hill climbing with the high-speed gear in clutch and the grade is so stiff that it becomes necessary to engage the hill-climbing gear, first release the high-speed gear and, after applying sufficient pressure upon the governor-button to speed motor, draw in the short lever.

Never attempt to engage two clutches at the same time. Be careful always to release one before another is applied. Maintain a cool head at all times, and master the interesting details of operation before venturing near brick walls and telegraph poles.

Upon stopping motor do not neglect to immediately turn off the gasoline and lubricating oil at the main admission valves over supply tanks. It will then be unnecessary to touch the gasoline valves at carburetors.

LUBRICATION*. — A matter of greatest importance is that the proper quality of oil be fed to the motor bearings from the main reservoir. Should an improper quality be used it is very liable to result in actual damage to the motor from clogging the wick feeds contained in float-box (A-17, B-16), and being too stiff to flow through the feed pipes. Damage will also result from using a

*See note on page 14

5

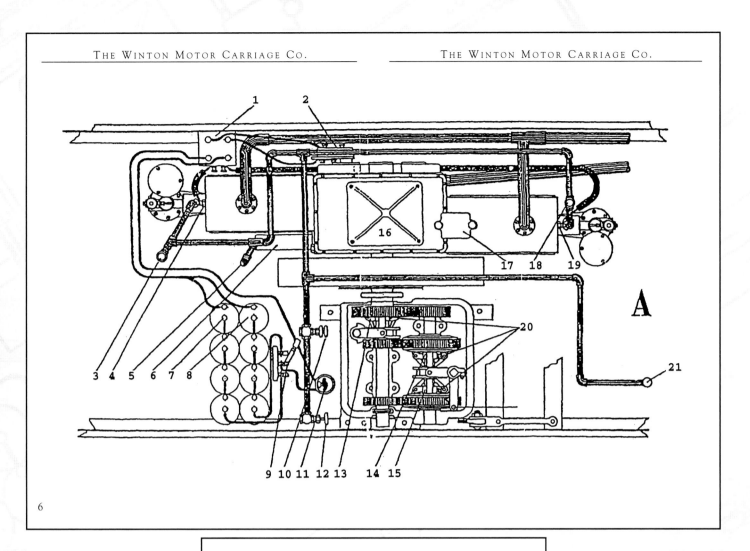

6

"A" REFERENCE NUMBERS

1 — Spark coil.
2 — Breaker-box.
3-18 — Oil cups for cylinder inlet valves.
4-19 — Spark plugs.
5 — Inlet for air pump.
6 — Air pump.
7-8 — Ignition batteries.
9 — Switch for alternating ignition batteries.
10 — Governor speed adjustment.
11 — When starting motor turn this switch to register "ON."
Switch should register "OFF" when motor is not running.
12 — Air line throttle. See instructions for starting motor.
13 — Adjusting nut for high-speed gear friction.
14 — Adjusting nut for slow-speed gear friction.
15 — Adjusting nut for backing gear friction.
16 — Cover box to motor crank case.
17 — Oil box into which lubricant flows from main oil reservoir before passing through the several pipes which connect with the motor bearings. If, at any time, lubrication is not perfect remove oil box cover and, if oil passages are in any wise obstructed, remedy the difficulty. Before motor is started for the first time remove cover from this box and inject a quantity of lubricant through the outlets which connect with the motor bearings.
20 — Set screws for locking friction bearings.
21 — Foot button.

7

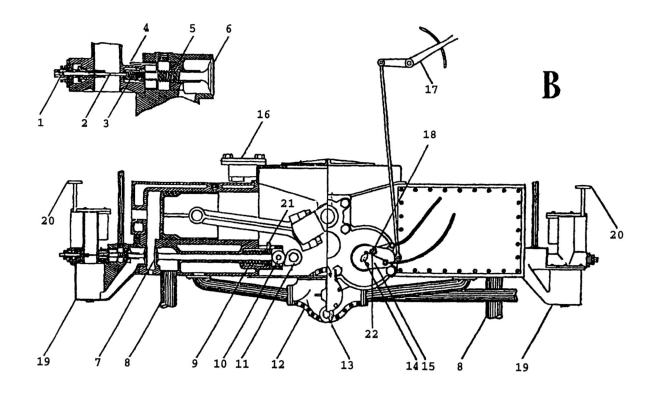

B

8

"B" REFERENCE NUMBERS

1 — Inlet valve needle adjustment.
2 — Inlet valve needle.
3 — Inlet valve needle spring.
4 — Priming stem. To allow starting charge of gasoline to enter carburetor, push this priming stem toward cylinder.
5 — Inlet valve spring.
6 — Inlet valve.
7 — Exhaust valve.
8 — Exhaust pipe.
9 — Exhaust valve spring.
10 — Exhaust valve roller.
11 — Exhaust cam.
12 — Water pump casing.
13 — Water drain cock.
14 — Spark cam.
15 — Breaker-box.
16 — Oil box (same as A-17).
17 — Lever regulating the time of spark.
18 — Screw adjustment for contact points.
19 — Carburetor.
20 — Valves which regulate gasoline supply to carburetor.
21 — Exhaust valve roller guide set-screw.
22 — Spark points should be firm in contact. *Do not turn adjusting screw down so far that undue strain is brought upon breaker spring.* When spark points are in proper contact there should be a scarcely perceptible bend in the breaker spring. A small set-screw at side of adjusting screw should always be retightened after making adjustment. The contact points are located, one upon the breaker spring and the other at the base of adjusting screw.

9

too thin oil. The one particular lubricant, which has been found absolutely satisfactory after exhaustive tests and severe experiment is Winton High Speed Oil. This should *always* be used in the reservoir to feed the motor bearings, and may be used also in the transmission gear-case.

We are especially anxious, however, that users of Winton Touring Cars do not make the mistake of adopting for motor use an untried grade of lubricant which some refiner or dealer represents as being "just as good."

If motor has been idle for two or more days, the main lubricating valve over reservoir should be opened five or ten minutes before motor is started. This time will be required to permit the oil to pass from the reservoir and down through the flat regulator to the motor bearings. Do not neglect this feature.

An oil pocket is provided at the bottom of the transmission gear-case. This pocket should be filled at all times and it may overflow to the extent of one-quarter inch depth covering the entire bottom of case. Do not allow a greater quantity to cover the bottom. Empty transmission gear-case occasionally and supply fresh oil.

Beneath the crank case is a drain cock. Open this every day and free the waste oil from the case. If any obstructing substance clogs the cock start the motor and the piston pressure will force the oil out without further effort on your part.

The differential gear does not require oiling at frequent intervals, but it should not be forgotten. To be entirely safe, unscrew one of the caps on face of differential drum and investigate every two or three days. If the gear does not give evidence of sufficient lubrica-

10

tion, inject into the drum the contents of one oil syringe, then replace cap.

The life of the driving chain may be prolonged by giving it occasional attention. Under ordinary conditions it will absorb enough lubricant from the transmission gears to serve all purposes, but should it at any time show dry, give it an oiling by using syringe. Lubricate it plentifully upon these occasions.

On the air line just above each carburetor is a small brass oil cup (A-3-18), equipped with a valve cut-off. Lubricant from these cups supply the inlet valves. Do not allow a cup full to feed to the inlet valve at one time. A few drops at the beginning of each day's hard operation will suffice. The contents of the cups will, therefore, last during several days' operation.

If daily operation averages 50 miles the front wheels should be oiled once in two days. To accomplish this, unturn the outside hub caps and a three-sixteenths-inch hole in ball retainer will be exposed. Inject through this hole a scant half-ounce of lubricant.

The rear axles revolve within roller bearings, which are contained in the axle yoke. Shifting surface oil cups are upon the axle yokes. Inject a small quantity of lubricant into the axle rollers daily, if service is continued and hard.

When it becomes necessary to make any repair or re-adjustment do not permit an inexperienced mechanic to "tinker." Direct your own repairs or satisfy yourself that the mechanic into whose hands your motor is given possesses the degree of knowledge necessary to insure the results aimed at.

Because the exhaust (B-7) and inlet (B-6) valves are so accessi-

ble do not allow them to be removed unless it is absolutely necessary. And if the valves are removed exercise the greatest care in replacing them.

To Remove Exhaust Valve.—Unturn the four visible nuts from the bolts which secure carburetor to end of cylinder. Disjoin the gasoline connecting pipe and lift carburetor from cylinder casting. The screw driver slot in exhaust valve head is then in sight. Unturn guide screw (B-21) back of the exhaust roller (B-10), then unturn exhaust valve until clear of holder.

To Remove Exhaust Valve Spring.—First release exhaust valve as explained above. The exhaust roller guide (inside crank case) is held by cap bearing. Unturn the two nuts, which secure the cap, then lift cap from bolt fastenings. With the exhaust valve freed and the cap bearing removed the roller guide may be lifted out. This renders the exhaust valve spring (B-9) accessible and it may be removed.

To Test Spark Plugs.—Unscrew the plugs from each cylinder and reconnect the wires in usual way. Lay the plugs upon carburetor float-boxes and, after removing cover from breaker-box, insert taper end of screw-driver between the contact points in breaker-box. Make and break the contact by movement of screw-driver, and then can be seen whether the spark is jumping at the plug points in the regular way.

Spark plug points should have 1-32 inch separation.

Do not use a spark plug upon which the porcelain has cracked.

To Adjust Gasoline Feed Needle.—When motor is not running, and the main and carburetor gasoline admission valves

are open, should there be a leak of gasoline through the hole in base of carburetor, it evidences improper adjustment of the inlet valve needle (B-2). It should be adjusted to stop the leak. To make this adjustment, turn up the adjusting nut (B-1) a quarter of a turn, or such additional amount as is necessary to stop leakage. Be careful about advancing this adjusting nut too far. Turn it ahead just enough to stop leak and no more.

To Test Motor for Gasoline Admission.—If the gasoline supply is irregular and the condition is indicated by uneven explosions, test the motor to locate the trouble. If too much gasoline is being admitted, the fact will be known by the exhaust of black smoke. If not enough gasoline is admitted, the exhaust gases will smart and irritate the eyes. To determine which of the two cylinders is giving improper results, test by closing the gasoline admission to one of the carburetors and run the motor on the single cylinder until, by the further opening or closing of the carburetor gasoline valve, the explosions of the single cylinder then operative become regular. Test the other cylinder in a similar manner.

Clutch Adjustment.—If clutches slip, when driving Car under load, release set screw (A-20) upon the particular friction plate adjusting nut needing attention (A-13-14-15) and turn the adjusting nut until the friction plates clutch firm when lever is drawn in. Retighten set screw after adjustment is completed.

Do not permit motor to race when clutches are slipping. Friction resulting therefrom may heat and destroy the effectiveness of the springs, which hold the friction plates apart when lever is not drawn in.

Chain Adjustment.—The regulation of transmission chain tensions is by means of the adjusting screws at the upper end of tubular reaches, which connect the sides of motor frame to rear axle. Release set nuts, then turn hexagons up or down as occasion requires. Do not throw chain out of proper alignment by turning these side set nuts unevenly.

After making the necessary adjustment, secure the set nuts at the upper end of reaches.

Brake Adjustment.—Uncouple turn-buckles at upper lever arms and give each buckle the necessary number of equal turns to insure the proper adjustment. When several adjustments result in bringing the threaded end of adjusting rod as far up into the turn-buckle as it will go, unturn the buckle to about one-half inch from the end of rod, take pin out of yoke on rear brake shoe and set up the coupling rod, which connects the shoes, one hole length.

Replace pin and complete the adjustment by taking up at the turn-buckle end. Treat both sides alike and be sure that when finished both sets of shoes work alike on the brake drums.

Note: (Referred to on page 5) 1904 car has a plunger oil pump operated by rear exhaust cam and housed in oil reservoir under crank case. Reservoir is filled before using the car by opening a valve in main supply tank under hood and shutting off the valve again when reservoir is full. Oil is forced from reservoir into sight feed located on top and rear of crank case cover and is regulated to proper number of drops per minute for the different bearings by adjusting the small screws on top of sight feeds.

Instructions for the mechanic were a bit more involved. . .

The Winton Control System.—The most conspicuous feature of the Winton Carriage is the pneumatic control system. The Winton system throttles the quantity of the mixture, the quality remaining always uniform. The throttle is actuated automatically by air pressure, produced by a small plunger pump secured to the rear end of the crank chamber and extending parallel with the rear cylinder. The pump piston is connected to the piston in the forward engine cylinder by a connecting rod, and the air pump, therefore, makes the same number of strokes per minute as either of the engine pistons, and each of its delivery strokes corresponds in time with a suction stroke of the engine. The pump draws warm air from the crank pit and delivers it into a pipe line leading to the two inlet valves. From this pipe line another line extends to two escape valves. One valve is the "set governor" for regulating the amount of fuel taken at even running, when the accelerator button is not depressed, and thus predetermines the maximum effect of the motor. It is operated by means of a dial lever at the side of the seat. The other valve is operated by means of a foot button under the operator's right foot. A spring holds the foot button valve on its seat when there is no foot pressure against it.

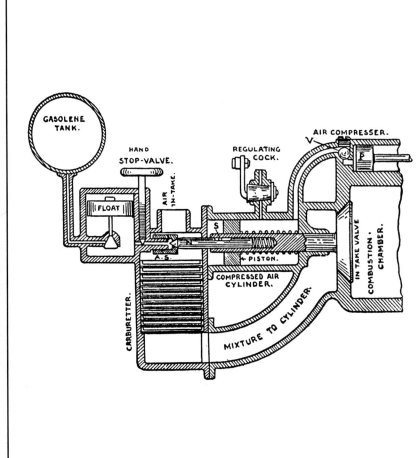

Fig. 283.-Diagrammatic Sketch of Winton's Carburetter and Intake Valve Action. The air compressor piston, P, is driven directly from one of the motor pistons, and forces air past the check valve, V, into the compressed air cylinder, where it operates to hold the piston to the left, and keeps the intaking valve closed, regardless of the piston suction tending to open the valve by moving it to the right. By means of the regulating cock the pressure may be reduced in the air cylinder, thus permitting the intake valve to open, more or less as the air pressure is more or less reduced in the cylinder. The needle valve, N, is seated in and carried by the intake valve stem, is spring pressed to the left by a coiled spring at its right end, is retained by a cross pin, S, and co-acts with the adjustable seat, A, S, to close or open the passage of gasoline from the float chamber to the carburetter underneath, whence the mixture is drawn to the cylinder through the intake valve. No gasoline can go to the carburetter without the motor piston is moved, and more or less gasoline goes to the carburetter as the intake valve is lifted more or less. The regulating cock governs the action of the motor by determining the amount of air that is allowed to escape through the vent. This cut, reproduced by courtesy of the "Automobile Trade Journal," shows only the theory, not the exact arrangement of the parts.

On the inlet valve in the carburetter is a small plunger, fitting into the cylinder to the right of spring, S, in the section of the carburetter, and between it and the inlet valve is a bushing that acts as a stuffing box. The air pressure leads to this small cylinder, and unless the pressure is relieved by opening either of the escape valves there is no chance for the inlet valve to unset and admit to the engine cylinder a charge of gas. On the extremity of the inlet valve is placed a conical needle valve, the taper of which is so proportioned that a lift of the inlet valve, allowing a certain volume of air to pass into the carburetter, will unseat the needle valve to admit into the carburetter a proper quantity of gasoline which, vaporizing and mixing with the air, produces the correct explosive mixture; consequently, no matter how great or small the charge entering the cylinder, the quality remains uniform.

With the air line entirely closed, the inlet valve cannot lift because of the air pressure against the plunger in the small cylinder. On relieving the air pressure by opening either or both of the escape valves, the pressure exerted on the plunger is relieved so that the inlet valve may lift correspondingly. The engine then draws a proportionate supply of mixture and reaches a relative speed. By pressing upon the foot button, the operator may relieve the air pressure by minute degrees from the entirely closed point to a point where the pressure in the air line is no greater than that of non-compressed air, so that the Winton motor is governed with extreme flexibility.

The air line may also serve as an automatic governor even if the "set governor" is but partially open and that the motor temporarily tends to increase in speed; the air pump, being attached to the piston, increases speed in the same proportion, and the air pressure is higher in the line because the area of the air relief has not been increased though the pump speed has. With the pressure increased on this inlet plunger, the valve will not lift as high, and throttles, thus bringing down the speed of the motor.

Assume the motor tendency to decrease in speed. The pressure in the air line will decrease because the pump is not working as fast as before, and because the relief opening has remained unchanged. As a result, the inlet valve will lift higher, allowing a greater charge to enter the cylinder, which will immediately accelerate the speed.

The above is an edited exerpt from:
James E. Homans, A.M.: *Self propelled vehicles A practical treatise on the theory, construction, operation, care and management of all forms of automobiles* (New York: Theo Audel & Company, 1905).

THE SURVIVORS

1903 WINTONS
Total Production 850 Automobiles

#1503	J.M.A. Patterson	England
#1684	Smithsonian Institution	Washington, D.C.
#1691	David Scott	Geddes, South Dakota
#1718	Conrad Fletcher	Golden, Colorado
#1868	Roger Allison	Fresno, California
#1951	Frederick Crawford Auto-Aviation Museum	Cleveland, Ohio
#2100	Peter Kesling Foundation	La Porte, Indiana
#2196	Allen Schmidt	Escondido, California
#2703	Luray Caverns	Luray, Virgin Islands
#N/A	Seal Cove Auto Museum	Bar Harbor, Maine

1904 WINTONS*
Total Production 600 Automobiles

#3042	Robert Robinson	Fresno, California
#3109	Edward Rowan	Far Hills, New Jersey
#3168	Manuel Souza	Wellington, Florida
#3227	Robert Stormont	Rockford, Illinois
#3452	Larry Hughes	Berthoud, Colorado
#3581	Nethercutt's Museum	Sylmar, California
#3602	Reynold-Alberta Museum	Alberta, Canada

The 1904 Wintons are included because they are almost identical to the 1903's. One major change was the addition of an oil pump in the crankcase to recirculate the oil rather than dump it on the ground at the end of each day. This improvement may have been prompted by Dr. Jackson's two major connecting rod failures due to the lack of proper and/or adequate supplies of oil.